CW00701803

ACCLAIM FOR *WHY DI*

'Whether you are the discoverer of an affair or the person who was discovered, Andrew G. Marshall's *Why Did I Cheat?* will help you gain insight and recover. His book covers information that people would normally need six months in weekly therapy sessions to learn and process. Best of all, in most cases, infidelity does not have to mean the relationship is over. If you are struggling with this, you must read this book.'

TERRY GASPARD, MSW, LICSW,
AUTHOR OF *THE REMARRIAGE MANUAL: HOW TO MAKE EVERYTHING WORK BETTER THE SECOND TIME AROUND*

'If you've cheated and are now facing the consequences, you need this book. It will take you firmly by the hand. It will speak equally to your heart and your mind. It will earn your trust. No one else writes with the same clarity, warmth, conviction, and depth of clinical experience. After finishing this book, my first thought was to go back and read it again. It's that good!'

STEPHEN SNYDER MD,
AUTHOR OF *LOVE WORTH MAKING*

ACCLAIM FOR ANDREW G. MARSHALL

'What he has told me has made me reassess
my relationship behaviour entirely.'

KATY REGAN, *DAILY MAIL*

'As if someone has just thrown a warm blanket
around my shoulders…it all makes sense.'

HANNAH BOOTH, *GUARDIAN*

'Marshall exudes calm; his voice is gentle and measured.'

TIM DOWLING, *GUARDIAN*

'Andrew G. Marshall offers deeply insightful, helpful, and
practical tools for dealing with most of the challenges we face.'

JED DIAMOND, PH.D.,
AUTHOR OF *THE IRRITABLE MALE SYNDROME*

'With advice on how to recreate intimacy while retaining a
sense of self… His insightful advice makes it hard to disagree.'

PSYCHOLOGIES MAGAZINE
(ON *I LOVE YOU BUT I'M NOT IN LOVE WITH YOU*)

'An insightful and gracious walk through
creating positive change in your life.'

ROBERT J. ACKERMAN, PH.D., EDITOR, *COUNSELOR MAGAZINE*
(ON *WAKE UP AND CHANGE YOUR LIFE*)

PREVIOUS TITLES BY ANDREW G. MARSHALL

I love you but I'm not in love with you:
Seven steps to saving your relationship

The single trap: The two-step guide to escaping
and finding lasting love

How can I ever trust you again:
Infidelity from discovery to recovery in seven steps

Are you right for me? Seven steps to getting clarity
and commitment in your relationship

Build a life-long love affair:
Seven steps to revitalising your relationship

Heal and move on: Seven steps to recovering from a break-up

Help your partner say yes:
Seven steps to achieving better cooperation and communication

Learn to love yourself enough:
Seven steps to improving your self-esteem and your relationships

Resolve your differences:
Seven steps to dealing with conflict in your relationship

Make love like a prairie vole:
Six steps to passionate, plentiful and monogamous sex

My wife doesn't love me any more:
The love coach guide to winning her back

I love you but you always put me last:
How to childproof your marriage

My husband doesn't love me and he's texting someone else:
The love coach guide to winning him back

Have the sex you want:
A couple's guide to getting back the spark

What is love? 50 questions about how to find, keep and rediscover it

Wake up and change your life:
How to survive a crisis and be stronger, wiser and happier

I can't get over my partner's affair:
50 questions about recovering from extreme betrayal
and the long-term impact of infidelity

It's not a midlife crisis, it's an opportunity:
How to be forty- or fifty-something without going off the rails

Can we start again please? Twenty questions to fall back in love

The happy couple's handbook:
Powerful love hacks for a successful relationship

ANDREW G. MARSHALL

WHY DID I CHEAT?

HELP YOUR PARTNER (AND YOURSELF) RECOVER FROM YOUR AFFAIR

MARSHALL METHOD
PUBLISHING

A Marshall Method Publishing Paperback

Copyright © 2019 Andrew G. Marshall

The right of Andrew G. Marshall to be identified as author of this Work has been asserted by him in accordance with sections 77 and 78 of the Copyright, Designs and Patents Act 1988.

All rights reserved. No part of this publication may be reproduced, stored in a retrieval system, copied in any form or by any means, electronic, mechanical, photocopying, recording or otherwise transmitted without written permission from the publisher. You must not circulate this book in any format.

Cover design by Liron Gilenberg ✦ www.ironicitalics.com
Interior design by Gary A. Rosenberg ✦ www.thebookcouple.com

ISBN: 978-1-9162745-0-1

Find out more about the author and his books at
www.marshallmethodpublishing.com

Printed and bound in Poland by BZGraf S.A.

For all my clients.
Thank you for all you have taught me.

CONTENTS

INTRODUCTION

This is an optimistic book. Although affairs cause a huge amount of pain, they also provide a great opportunity to learn about yourself, your partner and your relationship. And even though the couples who arrive in my office in the most distress are those dealing with infidelity, they're also the ones who leave the happiest. So why should that be? The other couples seeking my help know where the bodies in their relationship are buried – for example, she earns more than him or he hates her mother – but they tiptoe round these difficult areas and focus instead on the immediate problems that brought them into counselling. And that's fine, because nobody wants to dig up painful topics – so there's a spoken or unspoken contract: let's not go there. What makes working with couples recovering from infidelity particularly rewarding is they are prepared to roll up their sleeves and not only look at the dead bodies but give them a proper burial – in case they might continue to haunt their relationship. However, this is not the only reason I am positive about your recovery.

To be honest, I never thought I would write this book. I didn't believe there would be a market. Traditionally, someone who has had an affair wants to clean up the mess as quickly as possible and forget it ever happened. They certainly don't want to shine a light into all the dark corners of their life. However, over the last three years, something wonderful has happened. Men and women have started turning up at my office wanting to understand why they had an affair, willing to act on what they discover and committed to their own personal growth. Unfortunately, these clients all had the same problem. They had no sense of how to start this process, nor what questions to ask themselves, and if they did have some tentative thoughts no idea how to answer them.

There are lots of books for someone whose partner has had an affair. I have written two myself: *How Can I Ever Trust You Again? From discovery to recovery in seven steps* (Bloomsbury) and *I Can't Get Over My Partner's Affair: 50 questions about recovering from extreme betrayal and the long-term impact of infidelity* (Marshall Method Publishing). However, there are only a couple of books for the person who had the affair. They are normally religious and focused on shaming the 'guilty party', or counsel forgetting any issues he or she might have and focusing on helping their partner recover. I doubt anyone who has had an affair finishes the first kind of book – because they feel bad enough already without being lectured – and the second kind are fine (because partners need a lot of support), but it's only the first part of the journey.

So if you've had an affair and you're wondering what next, let me explain my programme to help not only your partner but *you* to recover and to rebuild your relationship (or separate on amicable terms). My main aim is for you to understand yourself better – hence the title *Why Did I Cheat?* You might feel a bit uncomfortable with this idea. Perhaps it sounds selfish to be thinking about your own needs and, heaven knows, you've been accused of that enough already. Perhaps you're thinking, I broke my partner's trust, so I should fix it. These are all legitimate concerns and I will address both of them in this book but first let me explain…

Understanding yourself will benefit your partner in a number of ways. You are less likely to be grumpy, react badly to his or her questions and explode – thereby setting back both of your recoveries. You will also be less likely to panic, lose all hope and do something stupid. For example, checking on your affair partner's Facebook page, which will inevitably be discovered and prompt a fresh crisis. I will also help you cope with *your* difficult feelings – like guilt, shame, remorse – so you don't get overwhelmed, close down or threaten to end the relationship (even though you don't really mean it).

Your partner will have different fears at different places along the healing process and you will need to respond in different ways. I cover all seven stages – starting with discovery – and how some unfaithful partners unwittingly blow up their marriages even though they are trying to save them. I will help you understand why your partner is so deeply hurt, the extent of the fallout from infidelity, and stop you from unwittingly saying upsetting things like, 'You're overreacting' – which just makes everything worse.

Perhaps you are comfortable with the subtitle of the book – 'Help your partner (and yourself) recover from your affair' – but worried about the main part: 'Why did I cheat?' The term 'cheating' puts your back up and it sounds like I am trying to shame you. I apologise. In the book, I talk about being unfaithful, infidelity and affairs. However, cheating is the term used in everyday discussions. Your partner will probably have asked, 'Why did you cheat?' and I needed a title that would attract attention, explain quickly what the book was about and did not have too much therapy-speak (which can be a barrier to many readers). Let me reassure you, I am not interested in shaming you. I believe there are two sides to every story and I want to help you fully understand yours.

If you have discovered that your partner has had an affair, you have my deepest sympathy. I hope this book will help you too. If you can't get your head round how he or she could have betrayed you, or his or her explanations make matters worse rather than better, this book will provide fresh insights. However, I need to warn you that it will not be an easy read. If you've only just discovered your partner's affair – and by that I mean in the last two or three months – I would suggest putting it down and coming back when you're completely over the shock of betrayal. (Please read *How Can I Ever Trust You Again* instead.) It is also possible that my approach will make you angry. So let me be clear: I am not interested in *excusing* his or her actions but *understanding*. So what's the difference? An excuse lets someone out of class and means that he or she doesn't learn anything – and as you will discover I'm very keen on people learning from their mistakes. Staying with the school metaphor, understanding helps to diagnose the causes of a problem and allows a proper assessment of which classes your partner needs to sign up for and the changes he or she needs to make.

I've been trained to listen to both halves of a couple and not to take sides, but that can appear as a problem after infidelity. We live in a blame culture – where if something goes wrong someone must be to blame (and once they've been uncovered a law suit can be launched to get damages). So while I'm listening and trying to understand your partner, it can be heard as 'letting him or her off lightly' or, even worse, 'blaming' you for his or her actions. If I give that impression, let me apologise in advance. I'm not interested in blaming anybody – it just makes people close down and that helps nobody. Remember I'm seeking to understand why your partner cheated and that will involve looking at how he or she was brought up. But, I'm not blaming his or her parents either, because they were, for example, critical and dismissive because they were probably judged by their parents too – and back through the generations.

Sadly, we also live in a culture that views infidelity as both titillating (with steamy soap operas and the vicarious thrills of celebrity gossip) and something so terrible that the guilty party should be metaphorically stoned (which makes it harder for the unfaithful to seek help and makes their partners feel 'wrong' if they are prepared to give him or her a second chance). Meanwhile, big business – in the shape of affair websites and pornography – is busy selling the allure of 'guilt-free' sex and even the idea that an affair can 'help' a marriage. However, there is no point blaming these people for exploiting human weakness. I might just as well howl against the moon.

So if you find this book hard-going, please remember I'm trying to understand how your marriage reached this dark place so I can help find a way forward that will work for *both* of you (because otherwise it will only be a temporary fix and what's the point of that?). If you are triggered by this book – by which I mean overwhelmed by feelings but it's not immediately obvious why – I apologise again. I've written a special appendix at the back which offers emergency help to address some of the reasons why you might be angry. Please turn to this section and see if it helps. If not, put the book down and wait until you're feeling stronger.

Don't worry, it's natural to be triggered after an affair. There are times when you just need reassurance and sympathy. You don't want to understand your partner, you just want to be understood yourself – and that's fine. Close the book and do something nice for yourself – run a hot bath, go for a run or play with your children. However, my promise is that when you fully understand why your partner cheated, you will be able to focus on what interests me most: how can your marriage become more loving and the two of you better connected?

Whether you are the discoverer of an affair or the person who was discovered, I want to offer one final piece of advice about my programme. I am going to cover issues that would normally need around six months in weekly therapy sessions. So don't be surprised if it takes time to absorb everything. If something doesn't make sense to you, skip over it. Maybe it doesn't apply to you or you're not at that stage yet. This book is designed to be your wise friend over the coming months, so come back to it when you're stuck or feeling down. You'll probably find the nugget you need second or third time around.

Finally, be patient with yourself. It takes time to recover from infidelity and it's going to be a tough but nonetheless rewarding journey. You're going to learn a lot about yourself – which can be a blessing and a curse. But whatever happens, my promise is that you're going to come out the other side a stronger person.

Andrew G. Marshall
www.andrewgmarshall.com

EMERGENCY RESPONSE

//////////////

CHAPTER ONE

WHERE DO I GO FROM HERE?

If you're reading this book, you will not be in a good place. You'll be racked with guilt. You'll be frightened. You won't be able to concentrate. Perhaps you have a small sliver of hope that I will help you move forward. More likely, you'll be worried that you're past helping and that there's not any good way out of this mess. I wouldn't be surprised if you're also feeling defensive. Especially, if your partner has given you this book to read and you're expecting a lecture on what a 'bad' person you are. So let me lay my cards on the table right away.

I am not going to judge. I am not going to shame. And I am going to try to avoid making you feel any more guilty than you already feel. My aim is to help you understand how you became unfaithful (either emotionally or physically or both) and to share my thirty-plus years of experience helping men and women – just like you – recover from infidelity. I will point out the most common pitfalls (in the hope that you'll avoid them or, if you do fall in, you'll climb out quickly), guide you through this crisis and help you out the other side into a better place. I hope I will stop you panicking or making rash decisions. When you're feeling down and hopeless, I will provide a healthy coping strategy – rather than becoming so low that you do something stupid and end up hurting yourself, your partner and the people who love you. It won't be easy but it will be better than closing your eyes and hoping for the best.

My recovery plan

Over my career as a marital therapist, I've probably seen three thousand clients and about half of those have been dealing with the fallout from infidelity. So I've heard about countless affairs and met lots of people who have been unfaithful – normally in the first few months after the discovery. So I have a good idea of what you're going through at the moment, the depth of the pain of your partner and the need to come up with a plan to get out of this dark place. So I expect you're aching to know how I am going to help.

First of all, I will help you clarify what you want so that you don't take the most painful path of all: bouncing between trying to save your marriage and pursuing the affair. Second, I will help you to help your partner recover from your affair so you're both in a calmer place and able to discuss what to do next. Third, I will provide you with the tools to tackle the question: why did I cheat? It's important to know the answer because unless you address the underlying issues behind your infidelity – both personal and in your relationship – there is a strong possibility that you'll only patch up your life and end up in a similar crisis a few years into the future. My goal is to help you resolve not only the immediate crisis of the affair but to lay the foundations for a happier and more loving future.

Do I have an agenda? I'm not going to try and persuade you to stay in your marriage no matter what. I haven't met you. I don't know what's right for you. I don't know your partner either. When we look at why you cheated, and discover things that need to change in your marriage, I don't know if your partner will be prepared to listen or not. However, it is only fair to say that I have strong beliefs. They are based on my years of practical experience working with couples recovering from infidelity and I will try to be upfront about them. So what are these beliefs?

It is important not to make any rash decisions about the future. Although you are hurting and want the pain to end as soon as possible, making promises that you can't deliver only pushes the problem down the road (where it will cause even more upset). Unless you explore the problems properly and fully understand them, you can't make a truly wise decision – you risk jumping out of the frying pan into the fire.

Next, it is important – from here onwards – to tell the truth. Unfortunately, you will have spent the duration of your affair telling lies – not only to your partner but probably your affair partner too. Worst of all, you have been lying to yourself – possibly for years: 'The problems in my marriage are not that bad' or 'I'm not *that* unhappy' or 'If I grit my teeth and get on with it something will change for the better'. Perhaps the lies to yourself have been about the affair: 'There's no harm in going for a coffee together – even if it is our little secret' or 'My partner won't be *that* upset' or 'What someone doesn't know can't hurt them'. Of course, a lie avoids a nasty confrontation; it can buy you time but it will make everything worse when the truth finally comes out. Lying can also be addictive and before you know it, you've told another half-truth. Worst of all, lies stop you from knowing your own mind and forming a credible plan for moving forward. So at the end of this chapter, I am going to ask you to imagine taking a truth drug. I know you will be doubtful. You're probably going, 'Yes, but…' or you're frightened of the consequences. In a second, I will address your doubts and go through some of your likely questions. But it is only fair to say that I will return to this topic over and over again in this book. It is lies that have got you into this crisis and as you'll discover, the truth is the only way out.

Should I tell my partner about my affair?

Perhaps your partner has been suspicious and been asking some awkward questions but you've been able to throw him or her off the scent by a combination of outright denial ('It's not what you think' and 'We're just friends') or simply going on the attack ('You don't trust me' and 'You're crazy to believe that'). Maybe your partner has *no* suspicions and that's making you angry; you've also tried to tell him or her that you're unhappy or 'I love you but I'm not in love with you', but nothing has fundamentally changed.

Reasons to keep quiet

I've heard lots of reasons why people are keeping an affair secret but basically they fall into the following categories:

➤ **I'm not ready yet.** You don't really know what you want. You're torn between your partner and your lover. If there was some way to 'have your cake and eat it', you would choose that option, and while you're trying to get your head round everything, you're putting off the decisions until some unspecified time in the future. Alternatively, you want to end the affair but you're worried about your lover's reaction, or he or she has threatened to contact your partner. In the meantime, you're living from day to day.

➤ **The affair is over and it meant nothing anyway.** It was a stupid mistake and you won't make it again. Anyway, it was a one-off. There was drink involved. You only kissed, so that wasn't really cheating (in your mind). Furthermore, it would be selfish to offload your guilt by confessing to your affair.

➤ **It avoids a huge amount of pain.** Your partner will be incredibly upset and he or she will want to go into every detail of your betrayal. It will not be pretty and you'll spend the next months (and possibly years) going back over everything again and again. Lots of people who have been found out (or confessed) will probably envy your situation and would give a lot to be able to turn back the clock and avoid the pain and heartache.

➤ **I have no idea what would happen next.** It could be that your husband or wife will get over the initial anger, be forgiving and agree to work on your marriage. Alternatively, he or she could be revengeful, try and turn the children against you and go straight for divorce. Even though you might think you know your partner, it is impossible to predict how she or he will react because you've not been in this situation before (and if you have, you don't know how much unresolved pain there is from the past affair).

➤ **We could still address the underlying problems in our marriage.** Few people cheat without being unhappy and having genuine issues with their partner. You could end the affair, tell your partner about these issues and go and get help to resolve them without confessing to the affair.

Reasons to confess

I understand why you are considering keeping quiet, but I believe the reasons for telling the truth are more compelling:

➤ **You will be found out.** Affairs leave a trail of evidence, texts, credit card bills, etc. It only needs for you to slip up once and your partner will find out. Alternatively, your lover's partner will discover the truth and tell all, or you could be seen out with your lover by someone who knows you. Worse still, it could be your son or daughter who will discover the truth and be left with a terrible dilemma. Even if you decide to end the affair, your lover might not agree and send lots of texts, maybe for months to come. He or she might become desperate and less cautious and even though 'nothing is happening' the evidence of past infidelity will come to light. (I've had clients for whom the affair came to light ten years later and the original hurt was compounded by the unfaithful partner keeping the secret for so long.) If you confess, you can choose the moment and how you tell. Although your partner will still be hurt, you have started to be honest and that will begin the long road to rebuilding trust.

➤ **You are minimising what happened.** By downplaying the extent of your infidelity or what it meant, you are also downplaying the extent of the problems that tipped you over the edge into infidelity or made 'no-strings' sex so attractive. If you don't face up to the truth about your unhappiness, how will you find the courage to change?

➤ **Couples therapy does not work with a secret in the room.** Once you can talk about something, you can begin to address it. If the affair is a secret floating around the room, it sucks all the air out of the session and couples counselling just goes round and round in circles without getting anywhere. I sometimes wonder why I am making so little progress, and then an affair is discovered (or lots of texting) by one partner and they bring the truth to the next session. In some ways, it is better late than never, but it nonetheless completely destroys the trust of the discoverer of the affair because their partner has been lying to them in my room (where they expect honesty). The unfaithful partner has also been lying to me (sometimes directly, sometimes by omission) and our relationship takes time to repair, too.

➤ **Your partner knows at some level.** It could be your partner knows everything and has been following all your messaging behind your back. At the other end of the scale, he or she knows that something is wrong and keeps trying to work out the problem but is missing an important piece of the jigsaw. If your partner asks: 'Are you having an affair?' I would always advise telling the truth. Otherwise, you have another black mark against your name when the truth finally comes out.

➤ **You can't do an honest appraisal of the situation without confessing.** In order to justify being unfaithful to yourself and still sleep at night, you need to tell yourself that you're extremely hard done by and your partner is an ogre or at least guilty of a long list of crimes. And it is amazing, when you start looking, how much you can come up with. But how fair is the picture you're painting? In the bubble of an affair, you can't take an honest look at your marriage or your affair partner.

➤ **Confession can be the trigger for a better relationship with your partner.** Infidelity makes couples dig deeper and learn more. You can't have your old marriage back but you can have a new and better one with your partner.

Post discovery: What are my options?

So you have confessed or been found out; your partner and you have probably talked more in the days and weeks since discovery day than you have in years – possibly ever. Your feelings are all over the place. One minute, you're crying along with your partner. The next, you're hugging each other. Another, and you're shouting at each other. You feel ashamed, frightened, hopeful, angry, guilty, loving and hurt – all at the same time. You will definitely be exhausted and you won't be able to concentrate on anything beyond the question: what do I do next? So let's look at the options:

Stay and commit to working on your marriage

Perhaps you knew all along that you would never leave your partner, being unfaithful was a big mistake and you will do anything to make it up to your husband or wife. Alternatively, you have been shocked by the depth of your partner's reaction to your affair. You didn't think he or she really cared. You have been moved by his or her vows to do 'anything to save the marriage' or by a readiness to forgive and work on improving your marriage. Congratulations. The road ahead will be tough, but with determination, a willingness to understand why you cheated and a commitment to changing, you will come out the other side of infidelity having learned a lot about yourself, your partner and with a stronger and more connected relationship.

Downside: It's easier to make the commitment to work on your marriage than to stick to it. When your husband or wife is completely distraught and you are the cause, you will want to make things better. Despite the recent evidence to the contrary, you're a great guy or a good woman. You want to dry your partner's eyes and take away the pain. The pressure building up inside you is so overwhelming, you need to fix everything – right now or at least by the end of the weekend. So you agree to stay and work on the marriage. And you believe every word, at the time. In fact, you are very convincing. You have lots of solutions – like changing jobs (because your affair partner was a work colleague) and a second honeymoon or taking your marriage vows again. Most likely, you're not just trying to convince your partner but yourself about this wonderful future.

Unfortunately, when you tell your affair partner about your decision, he or she is devastated as well. You feel terrible about hurting him or her, too. So although you *say* you're committed to working on your marriage, you are also trying to assuage your guilt about letting down your affair partner – after all, you told them you loved them more than the moon and the stars – and decide to keep open a back door to communicate.

Alternatively, you do make a clean break and stick to it – for a while – but you and your partner have a terrible row. He or she, in the heat of the moment, says, 'I will never forgive you' or 'I hate you'. Meanwhile, there's someone else who cares about you, who doesn't think you are terrible and will listen to your problems. Before you know it, you're back to having secrets again and, worse still, you're saying one thing to your partner and doing another behind his or her back.

Leave to be with the other man or woman

Your marriage was over years before you met your affair partner. You never knew that you could have such a deep connection with another human being. Your wife or husband is angry or grumpy or not interested in sex. The children will be hurt, but surely it's better that they have two happy parents rather than two miserable ones shackled together? Your husband or wife might not thank you now but one day, he or she will meet someone else. This option has the advantage of being clear. It also gives the impression of resolving everything as quickly as possible, and isn't that kinder?

Downside: Although you considered the marriage over, your partner thought it was alive and well (or possibly needing a bit of care and loving attention). He or she is completely and utterly destroyed. Of course, at some point in the future, your partner might pick him or herself up and make a new life but is highly unlikely to thank you or forgive you for ending the marriage. Your relationship with your children will also change for ever. Perhaps one of them will be open to patching things up, but there is bound to be another who is full of anger. Guess who they will take it out on? Yes, your new partner, and that is going to sour things between you. Furthermore, he or she will not want you to have much contact with your ex (and could also be uncooperative about another weekend with a moody uncooperative teenager). Raising children – even separately – involves lots of phone calls, texts and going to sports days or seeing teachers together. It can cause so much aggro with your new partner that you start omitting to tell him or her about all the contact. You are back to keeping secrets again and maybe even sharing confidences with your ex. (I have even had cases where ex-partners have sex again.)

Perhaps it won't even get this far; you will be racked with guilt about leaving and miss the children so much that you return home and try again. Except, you're still getting desperate or angry texts from your affair partner. You end up confused and miserable.

However, there is an even greater problem with leaving to be with the other man or woman. Rather than understanding 'Why did I cheat?' and making fundamental changes, you will find a superficial answer. For example: 'I was with the wrong man or woman.' Without looking deeper, once the honeymoon phase is over, you could easily be facing a similar set of problems with your new partner as in your original relationship.

Have time alone to get your head straight

You are not certain what you want. Your partner is promising a bright new future but you're not certain that you can believe in it. Perhaps your affair partner might be a better match but you're not a fool: you know everyday life won't be all moonlight and roses. There have been issues between you – but they have been avoided because you haven't been living together. Perhaps you shouldn't be with either of them? Maybe you need time alone to sort yourself out? After all, you are completely exhausted from trying to keep everybody happy. Your feelings are all over the place. You just want to catch up on your sleep. Perhaps then you'll be able to make a sensible decision and stick to it.

There is much to recommend this option. There is an opportunity to learn a lot about yourself. It avoids one of the biggest traps post-confession or discovery: leaping before you look. There is a chance that you will get the blessing of your partner (and if you're concerned about it, your affair partner too).

Downside: After catching up on your sleep and unwinding a bit, you will begin to feel lonely. You'll switch on your phone and there's a 'how are you doing' text from your husband or wife. Before you know it, you're sucked back into the everyday drama of bringing up kids without time to think. Perhaps your affair partner is having a meltdown and – despite promising to give you space – has left thirty-two messages. Alternatively, you feel lonely or guilty and you call your affair partner 'just to check everything's OK' and before you know it, you've agreed to him or her coming over to the hotel and you're making wild passionate love. Your partner *will* find out – because he or she is on high alert. Whereas before, your husband or wife put down your mood swings to work or the kids playing up, now he or she will suspect contact with the other man or woman. You will probably end up lying and your partner will turn detective and expose the truth (and put the worst possible spin on it). The results will not be pretty.

In order to make this option work, look for a structured programme – perhaps a retreat (where they take away phones and ban outside contact) or a course (where you look at your childhood and understand yourself better). It is quite likely that you'll need longer than a weekend or a week. So if you're considering this option, discuss with your partner where you will stay, what the rules of contact will be (with both him or her and your affair partner) and give a rough answer about how long you will need.

Bouncing around

Nobody consciously chooses this option; it is where you end up if you commit to making your marriage work, promise to cut off all contact with the other man or woman, but are unable to follow through. It is also what happens when you leave to be with the affair partner but try and keep your options open with your husband or wife. Equally, it is arranging for space to get your head straight but using it to spend time with your affair partner or to discover what living together would be like.

Downside: To keep all the balls in the air, you have to lie to everybody. When you are discovered, you make even more promises to keep everyone sweet. Before too long, everybody is angry with you and nobody trusts you. You're stressed, drinking too much, on the verge of a breakdown and you *still* don't know what you want. Sadly, you're too busy fighting fires to find the mental space for any serious introspection. Ultimately, if you don't make a decision, it will be forced upon you. In the best-case scenario, you will hit rock bottom and finally start to understand yourself better and make the fundamental changes that I'm suggesting in this book. Sadly lots of people, in a desperate attempt to feel better straight away, hook up with the next person who shows a bit of kindness and they learn nothing. Not surprisingly, it solves none of their real problems.

CASE STUDY

Charlotte and Spencer, both in their late fifties, came to see me after his affair with a much younger woman was discovered. The couple had been together since school and Charlotte was determined to save their marriage. She had listened to his message that she only communicated problems and all the joy had been sucked out of their relationship, and had already started individual counselling before they began their couples counselling with me. In the sessions, he complained about not feeling supported in his work – he had a high-powered job which involved a lot of travelling – and he spent most of the week away from home. At the weekend, he wanted to recover, and although Charlotte understood, she wanted him to play his part in family life. (They had a son who was seventeen and a daughter of twenty.) We had had three or four sessions discussing his ambivalence about counselling – he wasn't certain the marriage could be saved – and her constant suspicion that he was still in contact with his affair partner. I wasn't surprised when, one weekend, she needed to check something on his phone and discovered a trail of texts with the other woman.

'It was only a few texts,' he said, trying to minimise.

'And you met up for coffee once,' Charlotte said, 'at least that's what you told me.'

'But we haven't slept together.'

Charlotte looked out of the window. It was clear she felt he was still *in* his affair.

'She's young,' he tried to explain to me. 'She needs a lot of support. I've been like a mentor to her.'

'Only five years older than our daughter,' Charlotte snorted. 'How do you think she's going to feel when she finds out?'

Spencer did something next, which I see a lot. He promised to give up contact, try harder and focus on his marriage. But although he saw himself as choosing the 'stay and work on my marriage' option, I suspected that he was still bouncing about.

Not surprisingly, he was caught out again. Charlotte asked him to leave, the children were told and his daughter was so furious she refused to let her father drive her back to university. Our next session was focused on the theme of this chapter: Where do I go from here? I went through the options above, Spencer opted for time to sort himself out and we ended couples counselling. However, with his track record I don't think either Charlotte or myself believed it would shift anything.

Nevertheless, I arranged for him to see one of my colleagues – when I am working with a couple I don't do individual work with one half – but he only attended a couple of times. I guess he wasn't ready to look deeper at the underlying causes of his unhappiness, why he cheated, and certainly not to take the truth drug (I will go into more details about this later in the chapter). He was still too busy bouncing about. I was surprised to get an email from him about three months later. It was full of woe and asking if he could see the other therapist again. I arranged for her to contact him but he never made an appointment.

///

Surely there must be another option?

I wouldn't be surprised if you didn't find any of the four options I've outlined particularly appetising and you're desperate to find a different way forward. In my thirty-plus years working with couples recovering from infidelity, I've come across other solutions that people have tried. Let's have a look at the advantages and disadvantages of each.

Close down the whole painful topic

You have promised to end the affair. You're not in contact with the other man or woman (beyond an occasional sneaky peak at their social media accounts or bumping into them in the corridor at work), so really there is nothing for your partner to worry about. And anyway, what's the point of rehashing all the gory details? It just gets everyone upset all over again. You have owned up to making a mistake and you've had so much grief, you certainly won't go there again. Thank you. Now if you could both just focus on the future, everything will be fine.

Downside: I am sure this option is very appealing, but there are two major problems. Firstly, your partner is still feeling rejected and betrayed. Worse still, he or she will believe you don't care enough to listen to his or her pain. In effect, you are expecting your partner to sort him or herself out – alone. So in your partner's way of thinking, you can't really love him or her. You are only interested in your own feelings, and you're selfish too. Furthermore, by closing down the topic, your partner can't see how much you are hurting inside. So he or she will think you're cold and hard too. It's not a recipe for a good recovery or anything beyond a miserable co-existence, until your partner deems the children are old enough for him or her to file for a divorce or you have another affair or your partner has one instead.

Secondly, because you have put a stopper over the topic of the affair, none of the unhappiness that I've outlined can come to the surface and be sorted out. All the problems – both personal and in your relationship – will remain untreated. You will in effect have a zombie marriage. By which I mean, it looks like it is alive and stumbling along to outsiders but for one or both of you, something has died inside.

Wean yourself or your affair partner off the affair

You know there is no future in your affair but you're not ready to let go just yet. Perhaps if you see him or her a few more times – like on his or her forthcoming birthday – you can somehow manage a soft landing. The affair will truly be in the past and you won't be left thinking, 'What if?'

Alternatively, you feel bad enough about ending the affair – after all your promises of eternal love – that you can't face being a complete bastard and just 'dumping' your affair partner. Perhaps if you disappear in stages, you will make it easier for everyone. Your partner will understand – after all you've chosen him or her – while your affair partner is going to be left with nothing.

Downside: Your partner will *not* understand. He or she will deduce, correctly, that you're not really committed to your marriage. He or she will fear that the affair will spark up again at any moment. Maybe your partner will consider entertaining the plan – because he or she is desperate to save the marriage and this option holds out the hope, however illusory, of the affair ending – but he or she will be overwhelmed with despair. In my counselling room, when the partner who has been unfaithful puts forward this option, I only have to ask one question for it to evaporate: 'How is weaning off going to work in practice?' Of course, the partner having the affair is not going say to their husband or wife: 'I'm just off to see my affair partner, I'll be back home at ten.' Their husband or wife would be eaten up with fear and anger and either wearing out the carpet by pacing the room or out stalking the 'lovers'.

If you're considering this option, you will be continuing to lie and planning secret hook-ups. In effect, your partner will be on edge *all* the time – never knowing if you will return with a smile and a joke at the normal time or slink back home under the cover of darkness smelling of another man or woman. It would be the equivalent of torturing your partner. And there is one final problem with this option. *There is no such thing as a soft landing from an affair.* You either do the work I will outline later (and reach a better and happier future) or you shut down the topic (and keep the pain trapped inside you, your partner and your marriage). There is no third way.

Stay friends with the affair partner

Your affair was not just about the sex. You have a lot in common. You were really able to talk and provide support for a whole range of problems. For example, you were able to open up about the death of your mother or, because your affair partner works with you, your difficult boss. He or she really 'gets' you. Shouldn't you be able to have *friends* and, by trying to stop you, your partner is showing just how 'controlling' he or she is?

Downside: Of course, it's OK to be friends with other people. Later in the book, I will explain why I believe a lack of true friends – by which I mean someone to discuss feelings and share experiences with – is one of the reasons why men are so susceptible to affairs. However, I will be suggesting more male friends – not female ones.

I would also like to explain what I mean by friends. A friendship happens in plain daylight. I can invite my friends to my home. I don't hide how often we speak, what we talk about or what we're going to do together. My friends either like my partner or if the two of them don't entirely see eye to eye, my friend respects our relationship and doesn't undermine it.

Certainly, it is possible to move from being lovers to friends. I have made that journey myself in the past. However, there was a gap between the two states – time to mourn the loss of the old love, before becoming 'just friends' – but if I am honest, these have mostly been low-level friendships: exchanging Christmas cards, attending big birthday parties and other public events where I have been one guest amongst many. It has not meant an intimate tête-à-tête. Furthermore, it takes a break of at least a year – with no contact – and more realistically, several years before either party is ready to make this transition. Is this truly the type of 'friendship' that you're proposing?

Furthermore, you have only a certain amount of emotional energy and time – especially if you have a family and a demanding job. If you divert too much of your stock into a 'friendship', it will inevitably impact on your relationship. At the moment, when you are learning and rebuilding your marriage (if that's what you truly want), you need to focus on your relationship.

If you're being honest, you're probably trying to lessen the pain of the separation – either by avoiding it altogether (in which you're lying to yourself about your true intentions), or you're trying to wean yourself or your partner off the affair (which as I've explained is doomed to failure).

There is one more option

Hopefully, by now, you will have made your decision about how to move forward and breathed a sigh of relief. The road ahead will be tough but at least you have some idea where you are heading. But what if you are still torn in two different directions? Fortunately, I have one final option.

Buying time

You have just been found out and you're all over the place. Perhaps the affair meant nothing, it was just a symptom of a wider malaise in your relationship or your life. However, you don't believe your partner's promises of changing. You worry that your marriage is past saving or that there are fundamental fault lines and you don't have the energy to address them. You are being pushed to make your mind up, to commit to your marriage, but you don't know what you want.

Alternatively, you believe that your affair was the real deal and you don't know if you can let him or her go. However, at the same time, you have a deep affection for your husband or wife, the children you have together and all this history. You're asking yourself, is it possible to love two people at the same time? Surely it should be possible to have some time to make a proper choice rather than opting for one or the other out of blind panic or because of some ultimatum?

I am all for taking your time to make a proper decision. I believe it is important to *explore* all the options and *understand* the implications, before moving on to *action*. If you're truly stuck, I'd like you to read the whole of this book before making a decision. I'd like you to do the exercises and digest the experiences of the other people in the case histories. In the final chapter, I will return to the topic of being undecided. Obviously, reading the whole book will buy you time. Sounds good? I thought so, but there is one condition…

Downside: Human beings don't like uncertainty – especially at times of crisis. Your partner will want to know where he or she stands. Your affair partner will fear that you are about to abandon him or her and they will send multiple distress signals. You will have all these complicated and painful feelings and you'll want to make them go away by making a decision. So this option will not be popular with anybody. However, if you can cope with uncertainty, conflict and difficult feelings without rushing to the exit and instead stay and learn the necessary lessons, you will take a giant stride towards a better life (whether you stay with your partner or not).

However, the only way you can truly buy time, rather than just bouncing around, is if you take the **truth drug**. That's my condition. So what do I mean by the truth drug? You must tell both your husband or wife and your affair partner how you are feeling (with no editing out of 'kindness' or to avoid their wrath). You must answer everybody's questions about the affair and the state of your marriage to the best of your ability, rather than dissembling or hiding facts. In this way, your husband or wife can make an *informed choice* about whether he or she wants to stay married or not. Your affair partner will also be able to decide whether he or she wants to tell his or her partner what has been happening or, if he or she is single, whether to wait around for your decision or not. You need to be truthful with yourself too. Instead of running away from your feelings, by distracting yourself or keeping busy, I would like you to stop, look and listen to them. In this way, you can begin to face the reality of what has happened – without minimising, rationalising or compartmentalising (more about these in Chapter Four).

Finally, you will need to be honest about continuing contact with your affair partner. If your husband or wife asks where you are going, you need to tell the truth – rather than pretending you are working late or visiting an old friend. It is possible that your partner might ask you to move out because he or she can't cope with ongoing contact and will feel too unsafe. After all, you are texting and phoning the other man or woman from the next room.

As I have explained, this option will not be popular but it's better than further damaging your marriage by continuing to lie and although nobody will like the truth (least of all you), it will bring grudging respect from your partner and your affair partner, and allow you to look at yourself in the mirror. But before you opt for this path, I have one final warning. You will only be able to buy yourself a bit of time, so use it wisely.

EXERCISE: FEELINGS DIARY

Whether you have decided on a way forward or you're still up in the air, you will have a whole lot of complicated feelings. Perhaps you feel overwhelmed and not certain what you're feeling from one minute to the next. Maybe you're experiencing so many contradictory feelings that you can't separate one from another and you're completely overwhelmed. Alternatively, as you've spent your whole life intellectualising, ignoring or minimising your feelings, you're not certain what you're feeling. Perhaps you know what you're feeling and desperately trying to avoid these emotions.

Whatever the situation, I am really interested in your feelings. They are part of the equation for sorting out this whole mess and reaching for the better future I'm talking about. That's why I'd like you to keep a feelings diary from now onwards.

TIME	FEELING	TRIGGER

➤ In the first column put the time of day. For example: 7.30 a.m.

➤ In the second column put the feeling. For example: Guilty.

➤ In the third column put the trigger. It could be an event (for example, I woke up and saw my partner had been crying) or it could be a thought (for example, I remembered that I took my affair partner to Paris where my husband or wife and I had spent many happy hours together).

➤ Be careful not to confuse thoughts and feelings. Just putting 'I feel' at the beginning of a sentence does not make what follows a feeling. For example, 'I feel nothing is going to change' is a thought. What might the feeling be: hopelessness? Despair? Sadness? Put the feeling in the second column and the thought – which has triggered the feeling – in the third column.

➤ It is important to distinguish between thoughts and feelings. In a later exercise, I will explain how we are going to treat them differently. For the moment, however, you just need to have them in the right column.

You will discover that you have hundreds of feelings a day. Get a notebook and write them all down or record them on your phone. It will probably be hard to capture every feeling as it happens, but when you have a moment – for example, on the train – look back over the past few hours and fill in your diary. Whenever you feel overwhelmed, listen to your feelings – there are probably a lot of competing ones at the same time – you don't need to do anything about them, beyond naming them and writing them down. Keep the diary for a couple of days and I will explain in the next chapter how to interpret it.

//

What about my affair partner?

So what might be the reaction of your affair partner if you decided to leave him or her? To give you some idea, here is a posting on my website:

'I was in an affair for two years, both of us are married. One day there were "I love yous" and then, the next day, I was texted that he is too emotionally attached and conflicted. He deleted his email and text app and said goodbye. How can a person just RIP the rug out after two years, and over text too? Is it that easy to just shut someone out of your life? I don't trust my judgement. Is he sincere or just full of bullsh*t?'

If you are committed to working on your marriage or having time alone to get your head straight, you will need to tell your affair partner and end contact. Otherwise, as I've said before, you will be just bouncing around. What you will be hoping is that you will avoid the sort of confrontation in the post above. *Unfortunately, there is no soft landing.* Sorry. I can't give a magical set of words that will explain your decision, remove your affair partner's upset, allow him or her to give his or her blessing and for you to leave feeling OK. Personally, I don't think it makes much difference whether it is face-to-face or over the phone. It will still hurt – for both of you. If I had any advice, it would be the following:

➤ **Tell the unvarnished truth.** If you try to soften the truth with 'nice' reasons for leaving – like being 'emotionally attached and conflicted' – they will not ring true.

➤ **Apologise.** Don't just say, 'I'm sorry', but list what you regret. For example, 'I regret leading you on' or 'not telling you about…' or 'letting my fantasies run away with me'. It has to come from the heart and if you have no regrets, don't make them up.

➤ **Explain about future contact.** If you work together, explain what contact will be acceptable (e.g. work topics only, meeting when other people are around). If you don't, you need to give the clear message that all contact has to end.

If you have just confessed or been found out by your partner, you might like to discuss with him or her how to end the affair. Take plenty of time to talk over the options and be honest about your feelings. Try to avoid agreeing to everything your partner demands – to assuage your guilt – and, for example, telling your affair partner it is over with your partner listening in. In all likelihood, it will seem so cold and hard that you will end up having a secret second conversation. Unfortunately, this contact will be found out and your marriage will be plunged even deeper into crisis. So keep talking until you find a solution that is acceptable to both you and your partner.

What if I'm not ready to take the truth drug?

Hopefully you've decided on a plan of action for resolving the crisis of your infidelity and you're ready to take the truth drug. It will make a huge contribution to your partner's recovery. Although it might not feel like it, especially at the beginning, being honest will also be the foundation for your recovery. However, taking the truth drug is a big step and I won't be surprised if it makes sense to your head, but not your heart. So let's look at what some of your reservations might be:

My partner will leave me

George, forty-eight, had been married to Caroline for twenty years and they had two children together. She had been married briefly in her early twenties but had got divorced after she discovered her husband was a serial adulterer. They came into counselling after Caroline uncovered an emotional affair between George and a work colleague. He insisted that it had not gone further than kissing and cuddling, but Caroline still had her doubts – despite his continued protestations.

'But for months, you had insisted that it was just "talking" and a "special friendship" and that you "had feelings for one another",' she said and turned to me. 'It just didn't add up. You don't write the texts that she did if there wasn't something more.'

'I've told you everything now,' replied George. 'Promise.'

'Can you see why I don't believe you?'

'But I couldn't tell you the truth because you had always sworn that you'd leave me if I was unfaithful. I still can't believe you're still here but I love you and I want to do everything to save our marriage.'

My policy is to take what my clients say at face value. There is no point in having the same sort of circular argument in my room that they've been having at home, so I worked on improving their overall communication and understanding why George had cheated.

Advantage of taking the truth drug: Although your partner might have repeatedly warned that infidelity is a deal breaker, there is a big difference between what he or she might have said about a hypothetical situation and his or her actions faced with the reality of an affair. You cannot predict your partner's course of action. You cannot control your partner either – and beyond when you're panicking, I doubt this is something you really want.

In my experience, your partner is more likely to leave because you are holding information back or denying the physical evidence of your infidelity – like texts and bills. While the truth allows you to start again and become a team to solve problems, lying keeps you in two separate camps. In the worst-case scenario, your partner will feel you are 'gaslighting' him or her. The term comes from a play and film by the British dramatist Patrick Hamilton (1904–62) and is defined as trying to manipulate someone by sowing doubts about their memory, their perceptions and even their sanity.

My partner will be hurt

Sandra, forty-three, decided to end her long-term affair with a work colleague because the two of them could see no future together as the impact on their children and their partners would be too great. 'Making everybody else miserable was too high a cost. I couldn't live with myself,' she explained when she started individual therapy.

Although she had confessed to her partner, it had not significantly improved their relationship.

'I am angry because he didn't even notice that I'd been unfaithful – even though my moods were all over the place.'

When I asked how much her husband knew about the affair, I discovered that there was some important information that she was holding back.

'I haven't told him the identity of my lover because they know each other and I don't think it would be fair to burden my husband with that knowledge. The affair is over, so what's the point of hurting him further?'

Advantage of taking the truth drug: Your partner is not a child. Your partner is an adult who can make his or her own decisions about what information and what level of detail he or she needs. Of course, you can question that decision. For example, 'Are you sure you want to know what positions we used in bed?' However, if your partner believes that knowing this information is necessary, let him or her be the judge of it. For many people who discover infidelity, the most painful aspect is the secrets held between their husband or wife and his or her lover. It is only by knowing everything that they can begin to feel less excluded. My advice is to cooperate.

With Sandra, I didn't need to challenge her about not taking the truth drug. By seeking help for herself, she triggered her husband into seeking individual therapy, too. Not long afterwards, Sandra reported that he had demanded to know the identity of her lover, she had given his name and the two of them were looking for a couples counsellor.

I will have to face the full impact of my shame

Shame is one of the most uncomfortable of all our emotions and we will go to great lengths to avoid it.

'Who were you trying to protect, me or yourself?' asked Madelaine, fifty-three, when she and her husband Mark, forty-five, started counselling to repair their marriage after his infidelity.

'I'd hurt you enough,' he replied.

'But what really hurt was shutting down. I've never seen you look so cold.'

When Mark had reached crisis point, rather than taking the truth drug, he had given Madelaine a partial truth: 'I love you but I'm not in love with you.'

'I'd repeatedly asked if there was somebody else but you had denied it, over and over again.'

'I thought if I told you, it would become about my affair when it was really only a symptom of how unhappy I'd become.'

'And you think I would never have found out? You'd miraculously meet this new woman, minutes after leaving me?'

'I didn't want to hurt you even more than I had.'

'But who were you really trying to protect?' Madelaine asked again.

'It wasn't the other woman, if that's what you think,' Mark countered. 'If I'd stopped and really thought about it, I would have known that I was doing something that went against my values. I was ashamed and full of guilt.'

Advantage of taking the truth drug: If you have admitted the reason for not taking the truth drug is to avoid facing your own shame, it sounds like you might soon be ready. After all, it is more honest to admit to protecting yourself, rather than trying to sound noble by 'protecting' your partner.

There could be good reasons why you are so reluctant. In Mark's case, he was made to feel a lot of shame as a child. His parents' marriage had imploded shortly after his birth and he'd always felt responsible. Sometimes when my clients talk, I get such strong images that I have to share them. In Mark's case, I could feel the shame piled up in corners of the room – like dust – and the slightest movement would disturb them and we would all choke. Immediately, Mark started sobbing and sobbing. I had put into words how he had been feeling. However, when he stopped crying, he felt much better and we could begin our work together.

I accept it will be painful to discover just what you're trying to shut away, but in my experience trying to keep the door closed is always worse than opening it and facing the full truth.

What if it is true love?

Returning to Sandra, who we met a few moments ago, she had doubts about staying in the marriage and still felt loyalty to the other man:

'All the books say that affairs are built on fantasy and you don't know the real person, but we had a true connection. We worked together, so we were colleagues and friends before we became lovers. He was genuinely interested in how I tick, he helped me through an emotional crisis when my mother died and I supported him with his problems. Have we made a big mistake by giving up our relationship and trying to rebuild our marriages? What if my husband and I simply are not compatible?'

Perhaps you are less sure than Sandra and want more time with your affair partner to decide if this relationship is truly the right choice? Perhaps you're not ready to leave your wife or husband but he or she says you can only stay in the marital home – and thereby find out your real feelings – if you give up all contact with your lover? Maybe you are in such a dark place that you simply don't know what you want and are trying to keep all your options open.

If only I had more time, you tell yourself, I could perhaps find the right path. Coming clean isn't possible because you would be forced to make a decision right now and possibly lose 'the love of your life'.

Advantage of taking the truth drug: If you're not ready to take the truth drug, you're not ready. However, I would like you to still keep reading and to keep an open mind. In Chapter Five, I am going to talk more about love, how it changes over time and how our mind can play tricks on us. Of course, the feelings you have for your affair partner might be 'true love', but before you make a such a big change based on love to your own life, your partner's life and your children's lives, wouldn't it be a good idea to understand more about it? I hope this book will answer your questions, provide useful insights and allow you to move forward with your eyes open (rather than simply hoping for the best). At the end of the book, I will return to the subject of the truth drug and hopefully you will be ready then to make a decision.

I don't believe change is possible

After James, forty-one, was found out, he ended his affair and told his wife, Philippa, that he wanted to try again:

'Our kids have been unsettled enough by my affair,' he explained – they had three children, all in their teens.

'Our daughter is a real daddy's girl and she has been really upset,' said Philippa.

'It's taken a while but I am beginning to repair my relationship with her.'

I suspected that James was staying more for the children than out of love for his wife, but in the early stages of counselling – where I help couples explore why the affair happened and understand what needs to change – that is not a problem.

About a month into the counselling, a dark cloud seemed to follow the couple into my office.

'I discovered that James had met up with the other woman for a drink after work on Friday night,' Philippa said. 'I could tell immediately, something was wrong because he was in a strange mood. He became tetchier and tetchier and I kept asking what was going on? I sort of knew but I wanted him to tell me, or perhaps I didn't want to believe my gut feelings. But after a horrible weekend, I confronted him on Sunday night and demanded the truth.'

'I should have come clean earlier but I'm having serious doubts. I can't believe that anything will really change between Philippa and I. We've had problems before and we resolve to try harder and things are better for a while but we slip back into our old ways.'

Advantage of taking the truth drug: I would not be surprised if you don't think your marriage can change. Especially if, like James and Philippa, you were childhood sweethearts and have spent your entire adult life together. Of course, you can't 'believe' in my programme because I haven't spelled it out yet. But rest assured, I'm not interested in a simple patch-up. I want to get to the bottom of why this affair happened, teach you better ways to communicate and help you decide together if your marriage has a future. However, it will take time and teamwork. Your partner will only allow you time if you are being honest (because it is so painful being on high alert *all* the time). You can only work as a team if there is at least *some* trust between you (and that is impossible if your partner keeps finding secret contact with your affair partner).

Let me be clear: by taking the truth drug you are not committed to staying in your marriage. You certainly don't have to believe that it can change. You are simply going to tell the truth and if your truth is 'I don't know if this marriage can be saved' that's fine. Your partner might not like the answer, but knowing where he or she stands is better than empty promises.

If you're *still* thinking, 'Yes, but...' you will find the next exercise helpful.

EXERCISE: WHAT NEEDS TO BE DIFFERENT?

The regular way to solve a problem is to look at what has gone wrong and seek a solution. However, in the nineteen-eighties, businesses started to embrace an idea called Appreciative Inquiry (AI). Rather than fixing problem areas, AI focuses on building on what already works. AI practitioners believe this approach makes staff more creative, increases trust and brings out the basic goodness in people. By contrast, problem-solving just encourages blame and fault-finding. I'd like you to do something similar with your marriage. The key is to imagine – for a moment – that your marriage is fixable. Take four pieces of paper, copy the headings below, think of as many answers as possible and write up your discoveries:

➤ **DISCOVER.** What is good about your relationship? Think about the good times and high points together. What did you most value about your partner? What did you like about yourself? What qualities did your relationship possess? Probe deeper. What else can you write down about what worked, or still works, in your relationship?

➤ **DREAM.** How would you like your relationship to be? What is important to you? What do you care about? Try and make the dream as vivid and detailed as possible.

➤ **DESIGN.** What would help you reach these goals? What skills do you have to draw on? What qualities does your partner have that would be useful? How would you need to change? How can you help each other? What can you both agree on?

➤ **DELIVER.** What is the first step? How could you reach it? What else would help? How will you know when you have reached your goals?

If you have any negative thoughts or come up with problems, that's fine. Write them down on a separate piece of paper to consider later. At the moment, I want you to stay positive and, for the duration of the exercise, believe your marriage can improve. The task is to have a clear idea of what needs to change and the first thoughts on how to achieve the goal.

CASE STUDY

'I am a guy who has been married for ten years but together with my wife for twenty-five. Last year was a dreadful one for us: my father-in-law died after a protracted illness (I held his hand at the end – we were very close). My lovely mother-in-law has Alzheimer's and had to be put in a care home because she couldn't cope on her own. All this had to be managed through many trips abroad to the country where they live. My wife and I had a very stressful time. She is very controlling and angry at the best of times but during this period things were very difficult indeed.

'Also, during this time my own mum fell suddenly ill and was in intensive care for two weeks. I was by her bedside when they told me that she wasn't going to make it. Fortunately, she did. On top of this, our dog died in the autumn. I would also add that these events had been preceded by years of difficulty with our children. My stepson is twenty-seven and our daughter is twenty, both have experienced emotional difficulties over the years.

'In October, I was attending a cultural event alone (my wife was abroad) and met this most amazing woman who I completely fell for. It felt like a lightning strike. She was single, my age (fifty-two) and very attractive. I wasn't looking to meet someone but what followed felt like a complete emotional meltdown. I confessed to this new woman that I was married; we didn't start an affair but started communicating via text. We met a couple of times for coffee and I felt totally smitten by her.

'Six weeks after meeting her, I moved out of the family home and took my wedding ring off. I told my wife that I was leaving and that we were now separated. There was no time when I was seeing both women at the same time. I was quite particular that I didn't want to be unfaithful. The following nine months were a roller coaster of difficult emotions, threats of divorce, romantic getaways, depression, tears, financial difficulties, renting of crummy places for me.

'Later, however, I came to see that my new relationship had calmed down and that it posed all kinds of issues and problems around my new partner's children, who also had emotional problems! Furthermore, my new partner was always going on about friends who had hooked up with wealthy guys. I do pretty well but after a divorce I knew I would be considerably poorer! I found this talk unsettling. I loved her but I was starting to feel that I was just exchanging one set of problems for another. I found myself starting to withdraw emotionally.

'Two weeks ago, I told my new partner that I had doubts about our relationship, that I still have feelings for my wife and that I wanted to move back into the family home and attempt reconciliation. My wife does not know about my new relationship, which I have just ended, and we are planning to go to couples counselling.

'Is it best to tell my wife about this new relationship? She would be very upset. Also, have I had a nervous breakdown or something? I'm struggling to understand what has happened to me. I've had individual counselling throughout this process. I felt everything I was doing was justified at the time, but now I really wonder. Was I even encouraged by the counsellor to go ahead with the new relationship because it "felt right"?'

My reply

You have been through some sort of crisis – whether you want to call it a nervous breakdown or, what I suspect your wife would think, a midlife crisis. It doesn't matter. So what could be the cause? It's normally that someone's old life or how they have been leading it no longer makes sense. If I was to guess, it sounds like you pride yourself on being rational, and either minimising or downplaying your emotions. You describe your children and your affair partner's children as having 'emotional problems' and your wife as 'angry' – so I guess that you consider emotions as problems. Interestingly, you think your counsellor encouraged you to leave because of emotions – 'it felt right'.

Like many rational men – after your life stopped working – you have gone to the opposite extreme. Your life has become entirely governed by feelings and you have thrown caution and rational thoughts out of the window. To make a wise decision, however, you need both brain AND heart.

Should you tell your wife about the relationship? In a word: yes. Of course, she will be angry, very angry because she will blame you (and this other woman) for all the pain she's been through. However, she will also be relieved because how you've been behaving and why you've been acting (from her perspective) so strangely will begin to make sense. Plus if you're going to rebuild your marriage, it has to be based on better communication, openness and honesty, and keeping secrets will doom the project before it has even started.

EXERCISE: TAKE THE TRUTH DRUG

When you're ready to take the truth drug, I'd like you to find or buy a throat lozenge or a boiled sweet. Close your eyes and imagine, as you put it in your mouth, that the lozenge has magical properties. As you suck on it, imagine it spreading to every part of your body: your tongue, your brain, down into your heart and into your stomach. Picture the blood vessels taking it to every part of your body: your arms, your fingers, your legs, your toes. You are full of truth. From now onwards, if you are tempted to be economical with the truth, stop and remind yourself: I have promised myself to be honest. I can only tell the truth.

////////////////////////////////////

SUMMARY

→ In the aftermath of an affair, it is easy to agree to anything to make your partner feel better. However, if you can't deliver on your promise you will just increase his or her suffering.

→ There are only three viable options after discovery or confessing to an affair: staying and working on your marriage; leaving to be with the affair partner; or spending time alone to consider what next. Everything else is just bouncing around.

→ If you are evasive, edit the truth or just plain lie to your partner, you are also lying to yourself and making it harder to discover what you truly want.

CHAPTER TWO

////////////////

HELP YOUR PARTNER RECOVER

You have decided to stay and work on your marriage. You are committed to telling the truth. Congratulations. However, after the initial relief of feeling unburdened and knowing where you stand, you probably won't be in a good place. Rather than solving everything, it seems your decision has opened up a whole new set of problems.

You have been forced to face the enormity of what you have done, the knock-on effect on your children and the full extent of your partner's pain. Furthermore, once you have committed to trying again, your partner has the space to consider if he or she wants to stay married, whether he or she can trust again and if your relationship is past saving. Therefore, I won't be surprised if you're still anxious, overwhelmed and sometimes despairing.

It is human nature to try and get through these difficult times as quickly as possible and reach the sunny uplands of tomorrow. Most likely, in your rush to escape the darkness, you might be compounding your partner's upset and setting back recovery, and even making divorce more probable.

Fortunately, there is another way. It is built around exploring the feelings provoked by infidelity (rather than sweeping them under the carpet), understanding the source of both your partner's pain and what needs to change to rebuild your relationship (rather than reaching for a sticking plaster), and ultimately putting together a thought-out action plan (rather than making a few empty promises). In this chapter, I am going to focus on your partner, help you to understand the impact of your infidelity on him or her and explain what helps and hinders recovery.

Why is your partner so hurt by infidelity?

You knew your partner would be hurt by your affair – that's why you went to great lengths to make certain he or she didn't find out. However, you never expected your partner to be so devastated nor that your infidelity would create such a profound crisis that he or she is questioning everything.

Unfortunately, the pain goes beyond the obvious: jealousy, betrayal and disgust. Infidelity taps into a whole range of issues and beliefs that your partner will find hard to articulate and you will find hard to hear – after all, you feel bad enough already. However, if you don't understand the full nature of your partner's pain, you are more likely to fall into the traps that I outline later in the chapter and your action plan will be unlikely to address the real problems. So what are these beliefs and why does infidelity cause such an existential threat?

Love will protect us

The happy ending in fairy tales and myths is a wedding. The prince and the princess fall in love and live happily ever after. We know that real life is more complicated and you might know from personal experience that people fall out of love. Perhaps your parents got divorced or you have been married before. Strangely enough, this will probably mean you believe in love even more. The problem is not love itself but that your parents or you chose the *wrong* person. You are certainly not going to make the same mistake! You will find someone who *truly* loves you. Someone who will slay dragons for you and sing love ballads under your window. Of course, there will be hard times and there will be arguments but you will be OK... because love will protect you.

If we stopped for a second, we would realise that this belief is a comfort blanket. However much we love someone, it doesn't mean they always have our best interests at heart and it doesn't stop terrible things from happening to them. (I know from personal experience about the second possibility. My first partner died after a long, debilitating illness.) However, if we dwelt on all the threats out there in the big, bad, dangerous world, we would go mad. So we wrap our comfort blanket even tighter round us and get on with something important – like earning a living or raising a family. Unfortunately, your partner has had the comfort blanket ripped away and he or she is alone in the dark woods. If love is not going to protect him or her, what is?

What this means: Your partner has had the myth on which his or her whole life has been built destroyed. No wonder he or she feels 'my world has been turned upside down'. Through the fog of shock and despair, he or she is looking at two possible solutions.

Firstly, the problem is not love but you. Your partner chose a lying cheating toad, but somewhere out there is someone who will recognise his or her true worth and the two of them can live happily ever after. However, your partner is no longer a child. He or she realises that the real world is more complicated than Hollywood romantic comedies and mainstream entertainment – designed to soothe us at the end of a hard day – would have us believe. Furthermore, your partner still has all sorts of positive feelings for you. You have children together. No wonder he or she feels torn in two.

If you are lucky, your partner has been doing some research into infidelity. He or she has perhaps read one of my books or visited the more thoughtful recovery sites on the internet. The second option is that the two of you can build together a new marriage built on adult foundations – rather than myths left over from your childhoods. Of course, love is wonderful. Having a deep connection helps a relationship. However, successful partnerships need skills too. These include how to communicate effectively, how to negotiate differences and how to find solutions that work for both of you. Don't worry, I will cover all these topics later in the book.

I am how I am treated

Our identity is central to how we fit into the world. It makes us feel solid and settled. But it is under attack like never before. New technology is disrupting many industries and stripping away whole categories of jobs. For example, I used to get a large chunk of my income from writing for newspapers or magazines but the internet has decimated their business model. If I write only a handful of articles, am I still a journalist? (I am lucky because I have other sources of identity, but others don't.)

Old certainties like gender are also being turned upside down by campaigners who say that being a man or woman is not down to the genitals we were born with but a social construct, and should therefore be challenged.

Politics have become centred on identity and nationalism with almost constant debate about who belongs and who doesn't. People who have lived in a country for many years and brought their children up there are being made to feel like outsiders.

With this background, our relationship has become a source of stability and an oasis of safety… until infidelity comes along. Your partner thought the two of you had a special connection, no one could make you happier and therefore he or she was unique, prized and special.

What this means: In romantic love, the promise is to share all our hopes and fears and longings with our beloved. With infidelity, you are taking these treasures and bestowing them on someone else. It is your affair partner who is special and the only conclusion your partner can draw is that he or she is worthless.

Not only has your partner's sense of him or herself – and identity – been stripped away but he or she is questioning: who are you? As many discoverers of infidelity tell me: 'I thought my husband was so solid' or 'I thought my wife had principles'.

How can your partner reconcile his or her view of you – built up over many years – with this stranger standing before them?

Someone must be to blame

In many ways, this is one of the most insidious beliefs – not only for your partner but for you too. Worse still, as you will discover, it slots into other beliefs – I will outline shortly – which become an even larger obstacle to overcome.

We live in a litigious world. If something goes wrong, it must be someone's fault and once it has been proven who is to blame, legal proceedings can be started and compensation awarded. In politics, nobody puts their hand up and says, 'I was wrong', they blame someone else: the liberal elite, the mainstream media, international capital or the enemy (however they are currently defined). When it comes to infidelity, most people talk about the guilty party (who cheated) and the innocent party (who was cheated on). I find these terms unhelpful, but they frame the debate because we live in a society where someone is always to blame… and unfortunately that's you.

What this means: Everything about your affair will be viewed through the lens of blame. So when your partner has moved from what happened on to why you were unfaithful, there are bound to be problems. Even though you are trying to explain what was going through your head and the excuses you told yourself, your partner will hear it as blaming him or her for your affair.

However, there is a dark twist in the blame game. From time to time, your partner will become full of self-loathing because – in some way – he or she was 'not good enough' or 'woman/man enough' to keep you faithful. Why should this be? Let's look at the third belief and how it interacts with 'someone must be to blame'.

It's our job to make our partner happy

I went to my nephew's wedding recently and in his groom's speech he told his bride that she had made him 'the happiest man in the world'. Despite it being a bit of a cliché, a collective sigh went through the room. When my oldest friend got married – in his mid-forties – he told me his wife-to-be had promised to 'make him happy'. It obviously struck a chord because he had lived – long term – with three different women without feeling the need to get married.

'It's our job to make our partner happy' is powerful because we want to believe it is true. Making someone else happy provides purpose and meaning in our lives and it's great to think that someone else has our back, too, and is dedicated to making our life better.

Sometimes, there is a difference in how men and women interpret the task of making their partners happy. For example, men see their job as providing financially for their wives and women try to manage the personal life of their husband (arranging his social life, keeping in touch with his mother, and helping him navigate the office politics). However, few people stop and question this belief. Can you really make someone happy? If you can, is it really your job?

What this means: It is easy to see how this belief interacts with the previous one – someone is to blame – and deepens the pain of infidelity. If you're happy to accept the praise when things are going well, you have to equally accept the blame when things go wrong: 'My partner is not happy because I have failed!' Of course, your partner knows, in his or her heart of hearts, that this is not really true. There are a million and one reasons why someone might not be happy – for example, losing a job, or having a mother with a sharp tongue.

However, for each and every one of us, we are at the centre of our lives – the star, so to speak – and therefore we make ourselves the prime suspect for our partner's unhappiness and infidelity. I hear the same message from the husbands and wives of people who have been unfaithful over and over again: 'I loved my husband or wife. I did all these loving things and this is how I was treated.' They both rebel against the idea they are to blame and are drawn to it at the same time.

I would not be surprised if your partner alternates between being angry with you (for blaming him or her for your infidelity) and being filled with self-loathing (because at some level he or she believes that *it is* his or her job to make you happy).

A good partner really knows their beloved

With this belief, you are supposed to be able to read your partner 'like a book'. You are supposed to know his or her character inside out and how he or she is likely to respond in any situation. After all, you love each other. You are on the same wavelength. So if there was a problem, your partner *should* have known and addressed it early enough to head off the affair.

What this means: Your partner is feeling stupid. He or she should have put all the clues together and uncovered your infidelity much sooner. And the longer the affair went on undetected, the stupider your partner will be feeling. If he or she had suspicions but was deflected, he or she will feel even more of a fool for believing your lies.

Personally, I've never really understood why people feel stupid. 'Do you really think you should be routinely suspicious of your partner?' I ask. 'Isn't thinking the best of somebody, rather than the worst, something to be applauded?' However, I don't buy into the myth that a good partner 'knows' their beloved. Time and again, in my therapy room, I discover just how complex people are. It's not just the conscious layers but all the unconscious beliefs, our upbringing, and all the experiences we have half forgotten but have left their mark that drive our behaviour.

Sometimes, I even wonder how well I know myself!

A strong man/woman wouldn't put up with this nonsense

Our society worships strength, self-sufficiency and knowing your own mind. A strong man picks himself up, dusts himself down and gets on with his life. He certainly wouldn't be snivelling and asking for a second chance. He wouldn't be asking what he did wrong. He'd climb back on his horse or get the next train out of town: 'There's plenty more fish in the sea.'

Meanwhile, an independent woman doesn't need a man holding her back. She's not going to be one of those 'stand by your man' wives – like the women of those politicians or prominent preachers photographed with their husbands with a smile on their face despite dying inside – who protect their husbands from the full impact of his infidelity and end up being pitied by other people. No way – she is going to the hairdresser's, she's going to drop a dress size and show him what he's missing.

What this means: This belief has become so all-pervasive that if your partner hasn't 'dumped the cheater', it's because he or she is *weak*. He or she is probably also stupid – see the previous belief – to fall for your lies in the first place and certainly to believe your promises of 'not making the same mistakes again'.

I've counselled the partners of many unfaithful men and women who want to save their marriage but are too ashamed to tell their friends. They don't want to hear the chorus of 'leave him' or the half-hearted 'we will support you whatever you decide'. So when these betrayed men and women most need help and support, they find themselves isolated, alone and, because this myth is so strong, feeling weak too.

No wonder your partner will sometimes feel overwhelmed, and overcompensate by getting angry and lashing out.

Get on with your life

It's weeks or months since D-Day – what the popular internet sites on recovering from infidelity call 'discovery day' – so shouldn't your partner be doing better by now? Surely she shouldn't still be crying every day, shouldn't he have stopped being eaten up with jealousy? Put 'life is too short to' into Google and you'll be deluged with messages like this:

➤ 'Life is too short to stress yourself with people who don't even deserve to be an issue in your life.'

➤ 'Life is too short to spend time with people who suck the happiness out of you.'

➤ 'Life is too short to be anything but happy.'

What this means: If your partner can't 'get on' with his or her life and 'move on', it will add an extra layer of pain – not only is there the original devastation from discovery but a critical voice inside telling him or her to 'get with the programme'. In the depths of your despair, you might have even added your voice to the chorus: 'Let's put this behind us.'

As you're beginning to discover, life is more complicated than this belief would suggest. However much you might both want to 'get on with life', the pain is too great and there are important lessons to be learned.

Tread carefully. What might seem like a shortcut to you, could easily bring 'Get on with your life' into play, or one of the other beliefs, and compound your partner's agony. Next time you're tempted to try to rush forward, I have a mantra that I tell all my clients: *I need to explore and understand before I can act.*

EXERCISE: FEELINGS DIARY REVISITED

Reading about the common beliefs that make recovery harder will probably have been difficult. You will have had all sorts of strong feelings – like despair and shame – and it's quite possible that you'll be feeling overwhelmed. Hopefully, you will have already started to keep a feelings diary – as I suggested in the previous chapter. If this is the case, please write down all the feelings in your diary – naming them is the first step to beginning to process them. I will explain more in a moment.

However, if you haven't started a feelings diary, I would ask you not to read the next section. You will benefit less if you look at how to analyse the diary before you have kept it! (To recap – either go straight to the next section – Six Common Mistakes – or turn back to the previous chapter, read the exercise and start your diary.)

Look back at your diary and answer the following questions:

➤ What have you learned about your feelings?

➤ What surprised you?

➤ What impact did keeping a diary have on your feelings?

➤ What patterns did you discover?

➤ What triggered the darkest feelings?

➤ How did your thoughts impact on your feelings?

➤ What is the range of feelings? Are they all in the middle range or spread across a bigger range? What are the highs and what are the lows?

Analysing your diary

➤ Have you only recorded negative feelings or under-recorded positive ones? What impact is this having on your life?

➤ As I only asked you to record feelings – not to focus on the negative ones – what does this say about your general attitude to feelings? Could you have been brought up to feel that feelings are 'bad' or 'need to be managed'?

➤ How long did the feelings last? Not long, I would guess. Another feeling would come along – maybe not a nice one – but no feeling would get stuck for ever.

➤ When you look back at a weekend, for example, do you tend to label it with one feeling – like 'good' or 'bad' – while the experience of the feelings diary tells us that it would have been filled with lots of different feelings from all shades of the spectrum?

I hope that you have found keeping the diary interesting and help-ful (and that you'll continue to keep one). For me, the most important lesson is *no feeling lasts for ever*. That's quite a relief at the moment when you're feeling so many strong and painful ones. So I will say it again: no feeling lasts for ever. There is a downside to this – the good ones don't last for ever either. So if no feeling lasts forever, I'd like you to *accept* the feeling. It is a natural reaction to something that's happened. Furthermore, it probably has something to teach you. And remember, it won't last for ever! If you do try and push it away, it will probably come back stronger. So please *accept the feeling*. (You will probably find that your feelings are driven by thoughts too. I will explain what to do with thoughts later in the chapter.)

So imagine that your feelings are a river and you're sitting in the grass on the bank watching them flow past: 'Fear, shame, anxiety, but look there is hope, and, oh, more anxiety and a moment of pleasure too.'

Sit and watch and accept. You're not in the water-management business. You can't put a dam in the river and keep only the 'good' feel-ings. You can't paddle faster and move the 'bad' ones down the river.

Six common mistakes

You're full of shame. Your partner alternates between tears and angry outbursts. The two of you are having long post-mortems – late into the night – the slightest thing can set off an argument. Worse still, neither of you are sleeping well and your patience and tempers are at breaking point.

You are stuck in the Slough of Despond. (The fictional bog created by the English writer and preacher John Bunyan 1628–88. In his book *Pilgrim's Progress*, Bunyan's hero, Christian, is sunk under the weight of his guilt and his sins.) No wonder you want to pull yourself out as quickly as possible, but in your struggle to escape you are in danger of making six common mistakes and slipping deeper into the bog.

1. Holding back information

Your ex-lover rung. You missed the call. No message was left. You didn't ring back. Effectively nothing happened. Perhaps you work in the same office as your ex-lover and although you are not on the same team, your boss has seconded you both onto the same project and that's going to involve being in some meetings together. But you won't be alone – or at least it's highly unlikely.

Alternatively, it's information about the affair that you're holding back. Perhaps, your lover wanted to see where you lived and, at the time, you thought there was no harm in it. However, your partner has discovered some reference to the family home in some old text from your lover and is pressing for all the details.

Why you might do it: Your husband or wife has been doing much better lately. You tell yourself that the small amount of contact with your affair partner is no threat to your marriage. So there's no need to rock the boat. Alternatively, you hold back details of the affair because, in your opinion, they are not particularly relevant. To justify this to yourself, you exaggerate the amount of detail your partner is after. You tell yourself: 'She wants to know what we ordered in the restaurant and which table we sat at' or 'He wants to know everything we talked about and I can't be expected to have a perfect recall.'

Why you shouldn't: You are making a unilateral decision on what is best for your partner to know. You are picking and choosing what to tell. You are leaving him or her in the dark. Ring any bells? Yes. It's repeating the patterns of behaviour from your affair. Holding back information might protect you from being overwhelmed by shame but it lays you open to the criticism: 'You're selfish and only think about yourself.'

What's more, your partner is an adult and he or she can choose what information will be helpful for his or her recovery. He or she is trying to piece together what happened and make sense of it in his or her mind. Perhaps the detail is irrelevant but the only way to know is to hear it. Meanwhile, in your partner's head is the worst possible scenario. You didn't just show your lover the family home, but you invited him or her inside and had sex in the marital bed. Worse still, you are holding back information because you still love your affair partner or the affair is still going on.

Finally, it's pointless holding back information. The missed call will be found and destroy any green shoots of trust. If something doesn't make sense to your partner, he or she will keep going over the same story until you provide the missing details.

What's the alternative?: As soon as you get a missed call, send a text to your partner and tell him or her what happened. If you delay – even by an hour – you will find reasons to hold back.

Even if the work project with your ex is only a rumour, tell your partner immediately – rather than waiting until it is a reality. In this way, you are a team thinking about how to handle it rather that your partner being on the outside and having the news sprung on him or her at the last minute.

If your partner wants shameful details about the affair, remind yourself that you have taken the truth drug and tell all. In a small way, you will be making amends for all the hurt caused by your actions.

2. Minimising

'I didn't set out to have an affair.' 'It didn't mean anything.' 'We didn't meet *that* often.' 'It only lasted for four months' (when it was really five and a half). 'We only kissed.' By minimising, you are trying to say 'move along' and 'nothing important happened here'. If you look back at the previous common mistake – holding back information – you will see that it goes hand in hand with minimising. In fact, you are trying to cut the crimes into smaller and smaller pieces until instead of being sent to the dog house, you can be let off with a rap across the knuckles.

Why you might do it: You know why you do it. You're trying to defend yourself. You are overwhelmed with guilt and shame and you can't look at yourself in the mirror. However, there is a less obvious reason. If you look back, you have been minimising in all sorts of areas of your life. You have been minimising your upset, for example, about feeling ignored by your husband because he spends so much time at work, or by your wife who always puts the children first. In other words, it is an ingrained habit that's helped you cope with the ups and downs of life, but it is also part of what got you into this mess in the first place.

Why you shouldn't: Minimising doesn't work. It just makes your partner angry and attack harder and more often. Even worse, you're telling your partner that his or her upset about, for example, the kiss at the office party is not valid (or at the very best exaggerated). This gives the message: I am neither interested in nor care about your feelings. In fact, if you keep on minimising, your partner will give up all hope and start listening to the friends who tell him or her 'you deserve better'. Instead of deconstructing the case against you, you're adding to the case for the prosecution.

What's the alternative?: I want you to accept your partner's feelings. From where he or she is standing, the kiss *is* a betrayal. Show you have noticed the impact on him or her: 'I can see you are feeling betrayed and angry.' Don't worry if you have got it wrong – because your partner will correct you. 'Not angry but furious.' If that's the case, repeat back the feeling. 'You are furious.' This will help your partner feel heard and accepted. If you can manage this you will discover two things.

Firstly, your fear that acknowledging the feelings will make them worse is unfounded. The anger will not go away but it will drop from a ten down to an eight.

Secondly, you will be sending your partner an important message: *I love you no matter what*. I know that sounds strange but let me explain. It's easy to love someone who is being nice to us but not someone who is angry or upset. Unfortunately, when you withdraw from the so-called negative emotions, you reinforce a message – which everybody learns as a child – that some parts of us are not acceptable. By accepting your partners anger, you are accepting him or her. It is an act of unconditional love.

3. Debating with your partner

I can't tell you how often I get caught in the crossfire of a pointless debate. It might be about the difference between watching a porn movie (where the actors have long since left the set and gone home) and a private show (where a porn star will jiggle online to the viewer's personal tastes and instructions). I have sat through a debate about whether the 'affair partner' was a good person (with troubles of his or her own) or a low-life homewrecker. If I had ten pounds for every time I've heard some technical debate about whether numbers are saved automatically by the phone itself or by the owner, I'd be a rich man.

Why you might do it: As I'm sure you are beginning to realise, these common mistakes go hand in hand. After holding back details of the shameful behaviour – for example about your tastes in porn – you will be trying to justify your actions. Watching 'ordinary' porn isn't cheating and personal shows over the internet are OK because you were not planning to meet up with the performer. In effect, you are minimising again.

Why you shouldn't: Debating is pointless. I have never heard a discoverer say: 'You know, I guess you're right. I've never thought of it that way before.' No, they get more and more angry or upset and the debate turns into a row; and it never ends well.

Not only does debating involve a tour through all the painful details of the affair again, but it sounds like you are trying to *excuse* your bad behaviour. You're not taking your crimes seriously and you are certainly not taking your partner's feelings seriously. So what's to stop it happening all over again?

Even if you do have a good point – buried somewhere in the debate – it will be trumped every time by your partner saying: 'But you cheated on me and cheating can never be justified or excused.'

What's the alternative?: Take a step back and ask yourself: what is this debate really about? It is not about technology or the functions of a mobile phone. So go the heart of the issue – which is normally trust – and name it. 'This brings up your fears and that you can't trust me.' I know I am stating the obvious but your partner will take an inward sigh of relief: he or she is taking me seriously. Next, ask a question: 'How could I help to start rebuilding your trust?' This will prompt a discussion rather than a row.

Alternatively, ask yourself: why do I care so much about this issue? For example, why do I need to defend private sex shows? It is probably because you can't bear the pain that you've caused and you're trying to get some acknowledgement that despite watching porn, you're not a 'bad' person. However, there are better ways of showing this than debating – for example, by committing to adopt the strategies for helping your partner, which I unveil later in this chapter.

If you discover there is an important issue for you at the bottom of the debate – for example, about the quality of your sex life – make a note of what you have found out. I suggest that you put your conclusion to one side for the moment. I will return later in the book to tackling fundamental unaddressed issues between the two of you. There is no problem with looking deeper but your partner will need to be over the raw first months of discovery, and approaching the topic through a debate (which frames it in the terms of right or wrong) is seldom productive.

4. Coming up with a magical solution

When holding back information, minimising and debating make matters worse rather than better; but the pain is so great that you'll need to make everything better *right now*. So you come up with *one* action that solves the problems – at a stroke.

It can be a positive magical solution: 'I will quit my job so I don't have to see my ex ever again' or a negative one: 'Why don't we just call it quits and get a divorce'. At first sight, the problem is solved and everybody can get on with their lives again. But it takes only a moment of reflection to ask: 'How are we going to pay the bills if I'm out of work?' or 'Even if we split up, we have two children in common, so we're still going to have to cooperate over bringing them up and see each other at their weddings, their children's christenings', etc.

Why you might do it: When someone is minimising, I find that there is an equally unhelpful behaviour with which it goes hand in hand. I call it catastrophising. Instead of trying to minimise the pain by finding excuses, justifications or ignoring it, you swing to the opposite direction and blow up everything out of all proportion. The pain felt today is projected into not just the next few months but until the end of time: 'My partner will *never* trust me again' and 'I will *always* have my movements double-checked'. After you have taken a bad situation and maximised the fall-out, you will naturally need a BIG solution and hopefully one that will magic the pain away.

Why you shouldn't: There is nothing wrong with leaving your job or deciding that your marriage is beyond repair, but these conclusions should be reached after a full discussion and considering all the implications.

When you come up with a quick solution to close down the pain – you are probably going to promise the moon and the stars. Your partner – who is equally keen on feeling better immediately – will want to believe your resolution. You might even throw in a couple of extravagant promises to show to your partner (and yourself) that you mean business.

In the cold light of day, the magical solution will not look so magical. In fact, it will be impossible. You will backtrack. You will find excuses. You will hurt your partner all over again and ruin any last traces of his or her trust.

Meanwhile the original problem – for example, what to do about regular but necessary contact with a work colleague with whom you have had an affair – has not been addressed and is still festering away.

What's the alternative?: Accept there are no magical solutions. In fact a magical solution – i.e. having an affair in order to feel better – is what got you into the Slough of Despond in the first place. There are no shortcuts, sorry. Fortunately, you are committed to doing the work of recovery: understanding why you cheated and discovering what changes you need to make both personally and as a couple and putting them into action.

5. Getting angry

You are doing your best but you get scant recognition and even less thanks. Everybody is having a go at you. The slightest thing, and sometimes nothing at all, can set your partner into a downward spiral, and you're asked the same questions over and over again.

Why you might do it: You are trapped in the Slough of Despond. You haven't been sleeping very well. You have a short fuse. There are lots of immediate triggers for your anger and most likely a lot of long-term causes (which you've been minimising for years). While you are being constantly shamed, your partner is painting himself or herself as whiter than white. No wonder you snap and fight back.

Why you shouldn't: No matter what the cause of your anger: your colleagues for dumping their work on you, your ex-affair partner for calling your office or the price of potatoes… your partner will assume that your anger is directed solely at him or her. (Remember, in our heads, we are the hero or heroine of our own life, so if something happens we are not innocent bystanders but the prime suspects.)

To your partner, this is the final indignity. You are the one who cheated and she or he is being shouted at! Your rant, at the world in general, will be heard as: *blaming the victim.*

If you turn the anger inwards – 'I am so stupid', 'I did all these hateful things and nobody will love me ever again' and 'I can't do anything right' – you will be told that you are *'making this all about you.'*

What's the alternative?: Instead of ignoring your anger, letting it build up and exploding – what I call 'bottle and blow' – I would like you to accept, make friends with and understand it.

Be clear what you are angry about – it might not be just the immediate trigger. Be clear who you are angry with – it might not be your partner. Finally, ask yourself: what is my anger trying to tell me? It might not be as obvious as you think.

Instead of acting out your anger – by which I mean shouting, slamming doors and sulking – report it. Use this formula: *I feel... when you... because...*

By naming the feeling – in this case anger – your partner does not think it is something else (like hatred or contempt). You are also *owning* the anger: I feel angry. If you say, 'You make me angry' you are back to blaming your partner again.

By using the qualifier 'when you', you are limiting the feelings to particular occasions.

Finally, the word 'because' will explain the reasons – and they might be different from what your partner will assume.

It could be that you are angry about some particular part of your own behaviour. Your partner might know this but it will be good to hear it from your lips. You might even be angry with your affair partner. Your partner will be particularly keen to hear about this – because it points to an honest appraisal of your affair and shows it was not all wine and roses.

Reporting your feelings will also make them a little more manageable and help the two of you discuss the underlying issues rather than fight about them. So remember, the format is: *I feel... when you... because...*

6. Shutting down

You don't want to fight but you are being pushed to the limit. So you either physically walk away, go into yourself or agree to anything for a quiet life. Your partner will either feel that you are stonewalling him or her; or if you walk away, that he or she has literally only the wall left to address.

Why you might do it: The ancient and primitive part of the brain – called the hypothalamus – reacts to a perceived danger by triggering a 'fight or flight' response. It sends a signal to release adrenalin, quickening the heart rate, speeding the breath and preparing you to confront the perceived monster or run away. Although you can use the more evolved part of your brain, the pre-frontal cortex, to focus on combating this instinctive reaction, it is difficult. Especially when you are overwhelmed by high levels of stress today or old and unresolved trauma from the past.

Why you shouldn't: I wouldn't be at all surprised if shutting down is part of an established pattern that goes right back to the beginning of your relationship and stretches back into your childhood. It's probably how you dealt with being shamed as a child.

However understandable, and natural, shutting down might be — it makes your partner feel that you don't care and it can hamper the important work of learning from your infidelity.

What's the alternative?: The secret is to be aware of when you're about to zone out. If you speak up soon enough, while the pre-frontal cortex is still in charge, you can report where you are: 'I am close to shutting down.' You can also ask for a short break: 'Can I have a glass of water and a few seconds to calm down?'

Alternatively, you can negotiate a longer break but it will need to have a specific time built in to continue the conversation. I can't emphasise enough how important it is to stick to your half of the deal or it will be just another way of shutting down.

If you are able to ask for a break and then come back and resume the conversation, your partner will be less likely to pursue in the future. At the moment, he or she is frightened that this will be the one and only chance to talk.

CASE STUDY

I often get messages from partners of people who have had an affair thanking me for my books and telling me how helpful they have been in their journey to recovery. Sometimes, they tell me that their partners have been able to use my work to learn about themselves too. So I asked one woman if she would pass on my questions to her partner. Here they are along with what he wrote back:

What was happening in your life / How were you feeling in the run-up to your affair?

I was working and living away from home in another country and had been doing this for the last four years. We tried to make it that every seven to eight weeks either I would go home or my wife would come out to see me. This would be the final year of living apart before my wife and I would finally be back together, as I had been given a new assignment in another country and she was joining me on this one. I was finding living apart a real slog, especially as I had long periods on my own and the job was getting increasingly stressful. I met X on a night out with friends, she was flattering towards me and I could tell she liked me.

Looking back now, with all the knowledge you've acquired on your journey, do you have any idea why you were unfaithful and if so what are your thoughts?

I was lonely, I didn't have many local friends and missed the intimacy and companionship of my wife. It's also difficult to really talk to each other when only doing this by Skype, especially after being apart for so long and in different time zones. Having been out and met X, I was very flattered by the attention and we started to meet for lunch and to text one another. This was exciting for me. I also knew it was wrong but I couldn't seem to stop myself. I should have been stronger in not pursuing anything further, which is something I now deeply regret.

When you were discovered/confessed, how did you feel?

In some ways I felt relieved, like a big weight had been lifted from me. My affair and the deceit had changed my behaviours and I was struggling with not being myself and constantly having to cover things up. I felt immense shame that I could cause her such pain and anguish, not to mention damaging the life and love that we had shared together. This was an extremely hurtful period for both of us with a real uncertainty about our future together. However, I was clear that I loved my wife and wanted us to stay together.

How much of a full disclosure did you make?

Initially, I was reluctant to go into details as I didn't want to hurt my wife any further and was also ashamed at my behaviour. However, gradually I made a full disclosure including dates, times, places, etc., as this is what my wife needed for her to fully understand and frame it. She was very clear that I needed to tell her everything and didn't want any surprises in the future.

What do you know now that you wish you'd known then?

How much pain my affair would cause for all three of us. Not to sow the seeds by following up with lunch or texting because if I hadn't done this then it wouldn't have progressed. I would now talk to my wife and tell her of any flattering attention received. Affairs are not real life, you are living in a bubble and eventually this bubble bursts.

What advice would you give to anyone who has recently been discovered?

Be honest and open with your partner and answer all their questions. Take time out to talk to each other and don't make any rash decisions, give yourself time. Try to keep calm when discussing your affair. Stop all contact with the third party. The more people you tell, the more inputs and opinions you get, so think carefully about this.

Own 'your' affair, you did it – not your partner.

What have you learned about yourself?

How my behaviours would change in a way that I wouldn't recognise and what I am capable of doing. To recognise in the future when our relationship could possibly be strained and to talk about this. To be more open and honest.

EXERCISE: CHALLENGE YOUR THOUGHTS

When you look back at your feelings diary, you will find a lot of your emotions are driven by your thoughts. (If you haven't started a feelings diary yet, I strongly urge you to do so.) While my maxim is **accept the feelings**, I would like you to **challenge the thoughts**. If you look back at all the common mistakes, you will see that they are triggered by thoughts which have been exaggerated and, in some cases, blown out of all proportion. Here is how to do a reality check on your thoughts:

1. Start by taking dictation from that despairing voice in your head. Don't edit or miss out something (because you consider it preposterous), just write it all down. For example: 'My partner wants to know everything, no matter how trivial.' 'I can't be expected to have perfect recall.' 'My partner will never trust me again.' 'I'm doing my best but get scant recognition.' 'Everybody is having a go.' 'The slightest thing or something and nothing will set my partner off.' 'It was only a kiss.'

2. Look for all the exaggerating words: *everything* (your partner does not want to know everything, just what she or he hopes will build a picture to help her or him understand the affair) and *never* (I doubt your partner will be on his or her death bed and still talking about your affair) and *everybody* (it's unlikely that your brother or your mother or the man behind the counter at the local convenience store are having a go). Similar words to look out for are *always, nobody, forever*.

3. Next, work these sentences into something more accurate: 'My partner wants to know a lot of details.' 'It will take a long time for us to recover.' 'My wife, my children and my ex are angry with me (and my wife's friends too but I don't care so much about them).' How do these statements affect your feelings? My guess is that you will be less likely to panic or explode.

4. Look for all the minimising words. In the above examples of taking dictation from your inner voice, they are *only* and *slightest* and *scant* and *nothing*.

5. Rewrite the sentences with these words omitted or find a more accurate way of phrasing the sentence: 'I kissed another man.' 'I have had some recognition for my efforts (and last night my partner told me that our marathon session helped).' 'A lot can set my partner off (but that's because she has been hurt a lot).' My guess is that you will be feeling less self-righteous and more compassionate towards your partner.

6. Finally, cross out statements that are simply not true. For example: 'I can't be expected to have perfect recall.' The reality is your partner is asking for honesty and to stop holding back information.

///

Nine ways to help your partner's recovery

How you respond to your partner's upset will have a big impact on your partner's recovery. An affair gives the message — whether you meant to give it or not — 'I don't care about you, you're not my priority, you can't rely on me.' These nine techniques will start to address your partner's fears about the future and put your relationship on more solid ground today.

Listen

This is perhaps the most powerful technique of all. Look at your partner, nod your head to show that you are taking in what is being said, and from time to time repeat back the most important items that you have heard. For example, 'You felt really hurt that I spent so much time on the affair when you were crying out for some attention.'

When you are tempted to interrupt or justify yourself, bite the inside of your mouth instead. Monitor how often you need to use this trick — because it will give you an idea of how good you are at listening. As a rule of thumb, I would suggest two bites for every time you open your mouth.

Yes, but... I know it will be painful, you will want to make everything better and rescue your partner. Instead, you need to show that you *care* and you can do that by listening. You can double up the power of this technique by following it up with a question: 'Can you give me an example of what you mean by that...?' or 'How did that effect you?' In this way, you will show that you *are* interested in your partner's feelings.

Check in regularly

Your partner is anxious and will need a lot of reassurance. Small things, like being home ten minutes late, will trigger memories of the times that you disappeared for hours on end while you were having the affair.

To offer reassurance, send lots of texts during the day – so your partner knows what you're doing. Always flag up any changes in your agenda or hold-ups that could cause a delay. Send short chatty messages: 'thinking about you' and 'hope you are feeling better' and even something inspirational 'the leaves are coming out on the tree outside the window of my office which reminds me of new beginnings'.

Yes, but... I know it is a lot of work and you're busy, but your partner has probably seen the hundreds of texts to your affair partner. As I have heard lots of times: 'If he had time to text her, why doesn't he have time to text me?' By keeping in regular contact, you're sending your partner the message: you are a priority to me.

Be patient

Reporting in all the time is a lot of work. Having to account for your actions can make you feel like a child again. Your partner will have bad days when what seem to you random things will set off flashbacks (where the pain of discovery or the fear of not knowing what is going on is overwhelming). He or she will need a lot of reassurance and it will seem like a never-ending task. That's why you will need a lot of patience.

When you feel your patience running out, take a deep breath and another deep breath. Remind yourself that the period of needing extra reassurance does not last for ever. (I will explain the stages of recovery in the next chapter.)

Yes, but... It is natural to get angry if someone wants to go over the same story over and over. Worse still, if you remember things differently it will be seized on and blown up out of all proportion. However tempting it is to snap, I would still counsel patience. To your partner, getting angry equals something to hide. After all, during the affair, if your partner brought up concerns about how often you were texting a 'friend', staying out late or acting strangely, you probably batted away difficult questions by getting angry or going on the attack.

Show your workings

When I started my online support group for people who had discovered their partner's affair, I asked the members to nominate a topic that would be useful for me to cover. The overwhelming favourite topic was: how to get my partner to open up. Your wife or husband thought they knew you, they thought you would never betray them. They don't know this stranger lying beside them and that's frightening. So it would really help to know what's going on in your mind.

What do I mean by show your workings? When I was a schoolboy, my maths teacher drummed into us that there were only a few marks for giving the right answer, while the rest were awarded for showing the calculations for how you arrived there. Because I was rubbish at maths, I found it reassuring that I could get every answer wrong but just by showing that I understood the process I could pass the exam.

In the context of the affair, it is less important to come up with a final answer (i.e. stay or go) than it is to show what's going through your mind. Instead of keeping your regrets about losing your temper yesterday to yourself, tell your partner. If you are angry with yourself for not texting about the hold-up on the motorway, tell your partner. If you are overwhelmed with guilt about, for example, taking your affair partner to Paris, which had always been your city – tell your partner (even though you have told him or her this before).

Yes, but... I know you are frightened of opening up another long discussion, but your partner has become super-sensitive to your moods. He or she can tell when you're distracted, upset or depressed. (In fact, your partner always had a good idea when something was up but during the affair ignored, minimised or argued with his or her gut instincts.) If you don't show your workings, your partner will imagine your dark mood is prompted by a longing for your affair partner or even renewed contact. So although you think, by keeping silent, you are keeping the peace, you are probably adding fuel to your partner's anxieties and unwittingly prompting an imminent explosion.

What if the sadness *is* caused by longing for your affair partner and what might have been? I would still report it because it is better for your partner to know the truth – after all, you have taken the truth drug – than to be kept in the dark. If the sadness goes away after a day or two, which is highly likely, tell your partner about that too.

There is one final advantage of showing your partner your workings. You will be more aware of them yourself and that will lead to better decision-making.

Make 'no contact' mean no contact

When I started as a marital therapist, over thirty years ago, it was much easier to end contact with an affair partner. In the past, if you had wanted to speak to your lover, you would have had to sneak out of the house and find a public phone or wait until you went to work. Today, you carry around the means to communicate 24/7. If you have a moment of weakness, you can take out your mobile and send a message before you've had time to think it through. In the past, if you wanted news about your ex, you had to meet up with one of her friends or family or ask around at work. Today, you can look at pictures of his or her weekend activities on social media sites and updates about which restaurant he or she is visiting at any hour of the day or night. So the problem is not ending a relationship but keeping it ended.

Even though you might think a sneaky peek at Facebook is not contact, your partner will have a different take on it. Although you might still think you are committed to working on your relationship, your partner will consider it bouncing around, or even worse: 'You still love your affair partner.'

Yes, but... I know you can't control your ex and his or her activities but you can control how you respond. So while I had little advice on how to have the initial exit discussion, I have plenty to say about making no contact mean no contact.

➤ **Be polite.** When your affair partner sends desperate messages, don't ignore them — as this is likely to provoke more extreme ways of getting your attention. Send a short text back. Keep it polite and to the point: 'I'm sorry but I've decided to end contact.'

➤ **Don't get drawn in.** Your affair partner will ask for a proper explanation. He or she will hold out the possibility that if only you did a, b or c or told him or her what you mean by x, y or z that he or she will be able to understand, move on, or sleep at night. It is very tempting but I doubt that you will be able to deliver an explanation that will make sense to your affair partner or not provoke another deluge of questions. Your partner will find out about the renewed contact and accuse you (rightly) of breaking your word and destroying any remaining trust he or she has in you. So don't get drawn in, don't make threats, simply send your one-line response, restating clearly that you have decided to end contact.

➤ **Tell your partner about the contact.** I know your partner will be upset and there will be hours of recriminations. I know you won't want to rock the boat, especially when the two of you have been getting on better. However, you have taken the truth drug and that means not only telling the truth, but full disclosure of contact with the other man or woman. My advice would be to text your partner *immediately after* the contact comes: 'I had another text' and what you did: 'I did not reply' or 'I sent my standard response'. If you wait until you see your partner or you're less busy, you will come up with an excuse to keep quiet or maybe even forget (but remember, any contact *will* be found out). Your partner might like to read the message and discuss the pros and cons of this decision together. The two of you might also like to talk about when you will stop sending the standard responses. Don't forget, you can't control your affair partner but you are in control of your responses to any contact, and my advice is always to tell your partner — no matter what the short-term problems, it will pay dividends in the longer term.

Take full responsibility

Betrayal hurts so much that your partner will have turned not just to friends and family for support but will also be searching the internet for advice on what to do next. All the infidelity websites will give the same message: *your partner has to take full responsibility for his or her affair.*

So why does everyone consider this so important? We are back with the beliefs – which I covered at the beginning of this chapter – and how trying to explain why you cheated can be heard as: 'I blame you for my affair.'

Personally, as I don't believe that blaming people is helpful or that your partner is responsible for your happiness (your responsibility) or the state of your marriage (joint responsibility), I take it as a given that each of us is responsible for our actions. I don't think the phrase 'I take full responsibility for my affair/my actions' trips naturally off the tongue. It makes me think of a captain of industry – who has let private data be published on the internet – trying to keep his or her job.

However, I have seen in my therapy office just how powerful it can be for your partner. So I would recommend telling him or her: 'I take full responsibility for my affair.' In this way, you will reassure your partner that he or she is not being blamed. It allows the two of you to begin to look at difficult material without getting derailed.

Yes, but... I know that you could have legitimate complaints about your marriage or your partner's behaviour (even if you tried to resolve them in a destructive and illegitimate way). I know it sounds like your concerns are being closed down and ignored. Trust me, I have no intention of doing that. But for you to get to the point when you can look at the wider issues in your marriage – not just the period of the affair – the phrase 'I take full responsibility for my affair' is really necessary. In fact, I believe you can't say it too often.

Apologise

A fulsome apology not only shows that you take full responsibility for your actions, it expresses regret for the hurt caused and sends an implicit message that you will seek to avoid making the same mistakes again. What's more, a fulsome apology comes from the heart and expects nothing in return. So what's the difference between a fulsome apology and a normal one and what makes it so effective?

To make your apology into a fulsome one, it needs to have three parts. The first one is where you express your regret: 'I apologise' or 'I am sorry'. Next comes the key part: you identify the particular behaviour that you regret: 'I apologise for walking away when you got upset' or 'I am sorry that I texted my mistress during our son's first birthday party'. In part three, you demonstrate your understanding of how it affected your partner or why he or she is stuck on this particular detail of the affair. For example, 'I understand that by walking away I made you feel rejected all over again' or 'I understand the text effectively brought her into the house and made me less present at a key family time'.

So to sum up, the three parts are:

1. Express regret.

2. Identify the particular event or action.

3. Explain what in particular you regret.

Yes, but... I know that you have said, 'I'm sorry' a million times but you have probably undermined the power of the apology by adding an explanation (for example, 'I am sorry I walked away but you had really lost it') or minimising (for example, 'I'm sorry that I texted but it only took me thirty seconds'). The fulsome apology has only the three parts outlined above – no explanation. This doesn't mean that you cannot discuss the issues underneath your behaviour, but please leave them for at least twenty-four hours.

In most cases, you will discover your issue was really an excuse – for example, how long the text took is not that important (and you could no longer feel the need to explain). However, in my other example – the person who walked away because he or she felt overwhelmed by their partner's anger – this couple could benefit from a productive discussion about how to tackle sensitive and upsetting topics in a different way (which would allow the discoverer to share his or her feelings and the discovered not to be completely overcome with shame and guilt).

There is another difference between a regular apology and the fulsome one: it is the motive for the apology. In many regular apologies, there is an attempt to close down the conversation: 'If I say sorry, I can get my partner off my back and we can talk about something else.' By contrast, a fulsome apology is about acknowledging upset. It is not given with the expectation of anything in return – like forgiveness – but with an open heart.

As with taking responsibility, you cannot give too many fulsome apologies, but remember they must be about something specific rather than a blanket catch-all.

Bring up the affair yourself

When your partner doesn't mention the affair, you breathe a sigh of relief and enjoy the normality of your everyday life. However, your partner is left with the conclusion – probably rightly – 'If it was up to my husband/wife, we would never mention the affair again.' Worse still, he or she will draw the conclusion: 'It's up to me to rescue our marriage even though my partner was the one who put it in jeopardy.' As you can imagine, this thought will only add to his or her free-floating anger.

There are many ways to bring up the affair yourself. It could be by making a fulsome apology: 'I was thinking about my behaviour yesterday and (part one) I want to say I am sorry (part two) for getting defensive when you looked at my phone (part three). I understand it reminds you of how I acted during the affair and I have a long way to go before I can regain your trust.'

It could be showing your workings: 'I was thinking about our therapy session last week and how my behaviour during my affair has reminded you of how your father used to behave.'

Perhaps the most powerful option is asking a question: 'How are you doing today?' or 'I can detect that something is wrong, would you like to talk about it?'

Yes, but... I know that talking about the affair will remind your partner of his or her pain and trigger your shame and guilt. However, you will find the conversations initiated by you will have a different tone. Your partner will be grateful that you have brought up the affair, he or she will be more open to listening and the conversation will be more productive.

Even more important, you are becoming a team for resolving the affair and building a different kind of marriage (or if that is not possible, deciding together to separate rather than one of you imposing it on the other).

Commit to change

Your partner's greatest fear is that everything will be swept under the carpet, no lessons will be learned and therefore you could have another affair. The thought of experiencing this level of pain again is completely overwhelming and prompts a flight to certainty: we need to split up.

However, if you are prepared to learn from your mistakes, face your demons and change, your partner will not only be prepared to give you a second chance but can turn this negative experience into something positive: a better and more connected marriage.

Yes, but... You have no real understanding about why you cheated or what changes need to be made. That's perfectly understandable and something that we will address in the rest of the book. At the moment, you just need to commit to working on your marriage.

Perhaps you are not certain change is possible or whether you want to save your marriage. You are concerned that if you commit to working on your marriage, you will be leading your partner on – and that's not fair. However, assuming that you have children together, you will still need to be in each other's lives as co-parents. In this case, commit to working on your communication. After all, you have lots of day-to-day issues to resolve and it's hard enough, at the moment, when you're standing in the same kitchen. Imagine the possibilities for misunderstanding if you end up living separately and how much clearer you will need to express yourself and how much better you will need to listen. That's why work today on your communication is never wasted.

Finally, if you don't have children, I would like you still to commit to understanding how you got to this place – even if you don't know whether you want to stay or not. You can either use the learning to improve your marriage or to help you behave differently in your next relationship.

CASE STUDIES

Sometimes it is easier to hear what other people's partners would have found useful in the months after discovery – as it does not seem a direct criticism of you. So I asked my Infidelity Survival Training and Support Group for their input. Here's what they had to say:

➤ 'I would have liked some reassurance to help me feel more secure, as self-esteem was pretty low and my world felt more unpredictable. Things like offering suggestions that our phones weren't on in the evening so they didn't intrude on time alone. Something I'd asked for a long time ago. Maybe offering suggestions for a date or doing something out of the house without me having to prompt – like the cinema, a walk and drink along the seafront, a drive in the countryside, in a place he knew I loved the view, running a bath with my favourite bubbles – something that showed thought or bearing me in mind in ways that were personal to us. An affair raises questions that I am not in the forefront of his mind at that time, the OW is, and what helped for me at times was feeling his presence with me in moments he knew would mean something to me.'

➤ 'What was helpful was nothing too contrite or over the top, but little things that eased my distress at times. Being agreeable to chunks of time I needed to ask questions, and occasionally he would be candid and calm so that we could do that, then hug after and completely change the subject. Another thing that was helpful... he would suggest an evening walk together spontaneously and pick places I loved, then we'd stop off for a drink on the way back. He came to know that walking helped regulate my mood, so we did this often, sometimes in place of the gym. Next, he would pay for a class at the gym for me if he was going to be working at that time, and leave me a protein shake for afterwards, which was a sweet surprise. I appreciated him for it. Plus, he would bring a takeaway curry home so that I didn't have to think about cooking and put a favourite movie he remembered we both liked on the Sky planner. Finally, he bought me new bedding I'd seen in a shop. We were sleeping in separate rooms but I wanted a change from how the room I slept in looked, and really liked the look of some bedding. He also bought me a room diffuser with smells I liked.'

➤ 'Talk to your partner… no matter what you have to say. Do not leave the marital home… stay and communicate.'

➤ 'I wanted my husband to understand how I was feeling, to let me be angry if I needed to, let me cry too. I really wanted reassurance that he still wanted me, but to start off, he couldn't give me that as he didn't know what he wanted himself. That was really hard too and I don't know how that could have been made easier.'

➤ 'I asked a lot of difficult questions in the beginning about the affair and whilst many of the answers hurt and were really difficult to hear, I appreciated his honesty when, for so long, he'd been lying to me.'

➤ 'Be honest. Not to lie about things even if they seem minor. Take responsibility for the choices you made. Show empathy and try to help rebuild your wife's self-esteem.'

➤ 'We hugged when I said I needed it, but rarely spontaneously. I would have appreciated it if he'd offered more hugs.'

//

What helps and what hinders recovery in action

Mike and Sandra, a couple in their early fifties with two children, started therapy shortly after his short affair was discovered. 'Infidelity was always a deal breaker for me. I had a romantic view of love, I wanted us to be soul partners,' Sandra said as she tried to explain the circle that she kept going round and round. 'So I thought we must get divorced… but I love him. Except, is he really the man I loved because that man wouldn't have had an affair, brought the woman to our house and made our teenage son lie to me?' She would wake up in the night in cold sweats, going over all the horrible details.

After being discovered, Mike seemed committed to saving his marriage. He agreed to send a text to his affair partner – which Sandra and he wrote together – and Sandra began to come off high alert.

'I thought I could begin to trust him,' she said.

However, on a family holiday taken to start to rebuild, Sandra discovered a second phone and calls to the other woman (whose details he'd saved under his secretary's name). After a lot of cross-examining, Mike admitted to meeting his affair partner on a 'handful' of occasions for coffee. 'There had been no hand-holding or anything, just friendship.' After another huge row, he had agreed to block her number. Nevertheless, the other woman had sent another text and when this had been discovered, Mike had taken Sandra round to the other woman's home.

'I wanted to show Sandra that the relationship was truly over and I had nothing to hide,' he explained. (The affair partner had been angry, lost her temper and retreated back inside her flat.)

In the therapy session, Sandra wanted to go over parts of this story that 'didn't make sense'. She wanted to know if Mike was still holding information back from her. She feared that he still had 'feelings for the other woman'. Meanwhile, Mike wanted to close down the conversation because 'we have been through this a million times'. He also protested: 'I can't remember all the details and the timings.'

I am sure that you would recognise the cross examination that followed – because I bet that you and your partner have been round similar loops. So you won't be surprised that Mike fell into many of the common traps: minimising ('It's not like we kissed when we met for coffee or had full-blown sex') and debating ('I had lied to her too and I wanted to make amends to her because I felt guilty').

'So you had feelings for her.' Sandra burst into tears.

At this point, Mike got angry ('Can't I have friends?').

Sandra turned to me: 'This is why I fear that our marriage is beyond saving.' She was convinced that he was angry because he was holding back information.

Fortunately, Mike was able to use some of the positive strategies that promote recovery. He used a listening exercise (Reflective

Listening), which I will outline in the next chapter, and he was patient about going back over the painful details of his betrayal. He answered the question to the best of his ability – even though he thought the details inconsequential – and the mood in the room changed.

When I asked Sandra to examine what helped, she told me: 'I got new information. After we sent the first text, I asked time and again if he'd had a reply and he told me always no. It didn't make sense that she wouldn't reply at all.'

(Mike had explained that she 'had gone to ground' because 'I'd lied to her that I was separated' and indeed she had not replied for several days, but, by coincidence, she had sent a message after a particularly nasty row between Sandra and him. So he had decided to keep 'things warm' in case his marriage collapsed.)

'Furthermore, I now understand why she messaged even though we were on a holiday trying to rebuild our marriage,' Sandra explained.

(Mike had told his affair partner that he was away but gave the impression it was a holiday with his children only.)

'I have the date when the other woman knew the affair was one hundred per cent over and when Mike was fully committed to rebuilding his marriage,' said Sandra.

(It had been when Mike took her to the other woman's house.)

Until we had this post-mortem of the cross-examination, Mike had been despondent, and even afterwards he couldn't understand how it had been helpful: 'I didn't think I told you anything new,' he replied.

(It is possible that Mike could have told Sandra this information before but she could have been too upset for it to properly register.)

'Also, I can't understand how these small details really mattered,' he added.

'They matter to me,' Sandra replied, 'partly because I have been kept in the dark and knew nothing, so I feel I want to know everything. These details help me join the dots and tell the story of what happened in my head. Finally, it gives me reassurance that you're truly not holding stuff back any more.'

We finished the session with Mike giving a fulsome apology:

'I am sorry that I kept her "warm" because it destroyed your trust for the second time and set back your healing.'

SUMMARY

↝ How you respond to your partner's distress will have a big impact on his or her recovery.

↝ There will be times when your need for a break from talking about the affair will clash with your partner's need to understand what happened.

↝ In the first few months after discovery, your partner will be in such a dark place that his or her needs will often have to trump yours. However, this does not mean that you can't negotiate a break or ask to come back to the topic at an agreed time.

CHAPTER THREE

///////////////////////

HELP YOURSELF

Our smartphones provide us with both the means and the temptation to be unfaithful. As the US actor and comedian Aziz Ansari says: 'It's like a twenty-four-hour singles bar in your pocket all the time.' Meanwhile, society's attitudes towards infidelity have hardened and become more judgemental. So I would not be surprised if you are uncomfortable about the title of this chapter.

'I shouldn't be thinking about myself, I should be concentrating on making my wife feel better,' said Malcolm, a thirty-eight-year-old man who briefly left his wife for his affair partner. 'Especially after all the pain I caused her, for all the lies and still not coming clean even when she begged to know how I could be so cold and angry.' If you are nodding your head, please think of this chapter as a way of coping with your guilt and shame better so that you can be calm and patient with your partner.

Alternatively, you could be entirely comfortable with the idea of helping yourself and perhaps a bit angry too. Peter, in his early fifties, came to see me with his wife eighteen months after his affair had been discovered and the sexual element ended (but only a few months after he finally stopped his 'friendship' with the other woman). 'I get that I have hurt my wife and I am sorry, truly sorry, but does my affair mean that I have no rights going forward and I'm going to be permanently in the wrong?' My answer is that if your relationship is going to make a full recovery, it will need to work for both of you. So it's OK to help yourself — as long as it is not at the expense of helping your partner.

Maybe you are somewhere in the middle, and feeling lost and confused. Graham wrote to my website about his wife discovering his affair:

'I had never felt anything like it before. I was in a total state of shock. I thought I'd awakened from a nightmare – except I hadn't really. The reality of what I'd done, being faced with all the facts. It was horrendous and went against everything I thought I'd believed in. I had let down my wife, betrayed her trust so utterly. And at a secondary level too, I had lied to friends, relations, anyone who could have helped me. I had so much explaining to do at work, at home, in every walk of my life. I had no idea where to start, who to turn to. I wanted help badly but felt that there was none.'

Often I discover that men like Graham are expecting their wives to not only sort out their own pain but to help them navigate a way through theirs too. If you recognise yourself in this category, this chapter will help you, and we're back to that phrase again: 'Take responsibility'.

Seven stages of recovery

When you're stuck in the trenches of post-affair discovery, it's difficult to see past the immediate agony, anger and almost daily ambushes (with endless questions about what you did, what you said and what it means). It is easy to imagine that the pain will be at this intensity for ever – or at least well into the immediate future. That's why it's helpful to understand recovery moves through the following seven stages.

Stage One: Shock and disbelief

Your partner has been cocooned by the comforting myths about love. He or she has never been unfaithful and has no reason to think you would be. If your partner *has* entertained doubts recently, he or she has pushed them away or allowed you to squash them. 'The only way I could start to explain the pain to my husband of discovering his cheating,' explained Gretchen, the wife of Peter who we have just met, 'is to liken it to childbirth. I had no control over these intense feelings, they just swept through my body and I couldn't stop them. So frightening.'

Even though you know about the affair, and have full knowledge of the facts, you will go through this first stage too. Your emotions will also be all over the place. You had no idea that your partner would be this distraught. You were so busy pumping up your unhappiness (to justify your behaviour) and minimising the level of contact and intensity of the affair (so you could put it into a separate watertight box that didn't impact on the rest of your life) that you can't get your head round the reality of what you have done, how much you have hurt your partner, and the emptiness of the justifications for such emotional carnage. Just like your husband or wife, you are in shock and disbelief.

Stage Two: Intense questioning

Your partner will want to know everything that happened during the affair. Your partner will want to read your texts and emails. He or she will have lots and lots of questions. 'Although I told her pretty much everything, I just wanted to forget,' explained Graham who we met earlier. 'But she kept wanting all the fine details of where we had stayed, where we had sex, what sex we had had. The email accounts with which I had communicated, the emails themselves, the text messages, the poetry I sent her. It was awful bringing it all back up and I'm still not sure it helped particularly.'

To a lesser extent, you will be in the intense questioning stage, too. Your partner's questions, particularly about why, will force you to ask yourself some uncomfortable questions. It is highly likely that you struggle to make sense of your own behaviour. It is unlikely that your partner will find your answers either acceptable or understandable – prompting another round of questions.

Stage Three: Decision time

If you show genuine remorse and cooperate as your partner tries to piece together what happened during the affair, the damage to your relationship and the impact on his or her love for you, your partner will begin to entertain the idea of trying again. However, don't be surprised if the decision is ambiguous: 'I want to save our marriage but I don't know how I am ever going to trust you again.'

It is perfectly possible that one dark night your partner will declare the relationship over but in the morning light want to try again. I know it is hard to deal with these 180-degree turns, but even if you are thrown out and told never to return, please do not contact your affair partner or even worse, go round there. (Unless you are 100 per cent certain that you want to get divorced.) More than likely, your partner is expressing his or her anger, fear and despair.

Don't panic and set back your recovery. Stay at your mother's, your brother's or a hotel for a few nights. You can think longer term when both of you have calmed down and talked further. I hate to bring up an aphorism of my grandmother's, but 'act in haste and repent at leisure'.

Stage Four: Hope

Eventually your heart will stop racing, the conversations late into the night will take a turn for the better and you might enjoy the most passionate and connected sex in years. It is an unfamiliar feeling but slowly you begin to think it might be possible to work this out. Enjoy it while it lasts but be warned that hope is probably only a flicker at this stage.

Stage Five: Attempted normality

Hope feels so good that you will want to stay there. So you tiptoe around each other. Welcome to the fifth stage: Attempted normality. Your partner will try not to bring up the affair because he or she knows it will exasperate you and wants to forget, too. You will be on your best behaviour, joyfully doing all the chores that your partner has always wanted, and the children will breathe a sigh of relief. However, you both know this is an act. What my clients often call 'playing at happy families' or 'papering over the cracks'.

Consider attempted normality a staging post because without understanding why the affair happened and having a proper plan for what needs to change, you will be stuck somewhere between your old marriage (which died with the discovery of your affair) and a new marriage (built on everything you are going to learn and the changes you are going to implement).

Sadly, many people who've had affairs cling to attempted normality – don't complete the rest of the stages – and get stuck in a zombie marriage.

Stage Six: Despair – Bodies float to the surface

You are not going to like this stage. All the difficult conversations that you've avoided for years, the issues that have been settled with a compromise that worked for neither of you, and the painful stuff from your childhood will come sharply into focus. It's not going to be pretty but from a therapist's point of view this material is gold dust. Instead of running away, distracting yourself or going for a quick feel-good fix, you have the opportunity to sort everything out – for once and for all.

'But what's so wrong with having a "happy" life and just letting all this stuff sink back to the bottom of the murky pond?' asked Candy – one half of a lesbian couple who came to me for counselling.

'Because the result is either depression (because that's what happens when you suppress your feelings) or overworking (which leads to burn-out) or addiction (because you need more and more of a buzz to dull the pain),' I replied.

'That's pretty much what my partner has done,' she sighed.

There's a positive side too. When you stop running and turn to face these painful feelings – I will explain how shortly – they are not so scary after all. With some simple communication skills – explained in Chapter Seven – the problems are not so insoluble either.

Stage Seven: Intense learning

Instead of just circling round the same information and the same feelings, you begin to understand both the personal and relationship issues from infidelity. All the talking, accepting each other's feelings and challenging the thoughts (so there is less minimising or catastrophising) leads to better communication. You start to put together an action plan for the future based on a true understanding of what went wrong and what needs to change. Being more honest about your feelings and truly listening to each other – the heart of good communication – will not only help resolve deeply ingrained issues but deal with the new ones that life will inevitably throw up.

It is probably only at this last stage that your partner's trust will return. It takes time to demonstrate you are no longer holding back information and there are no more nasty shocks in the wings. More importantly, you understand why the affair happened and have developed the skills and a strategy to head off any future temptation.

Climbing up, falling down and getting stuck

I hope the seven stages of recovery sound good – as if there is a plan for moving on. However, I should warn you that it is not a straightforward journey. You can climb up the recovery ladder but new discoveries can also send you sliding back down.

'I told the other woman that it was over and she said that she understood,' said Graham. 'She then tried to contact me by telephone, text message and email for the next three to four months. I set up blocks on my email account but she changed her email address. I got a digital telephone for home that could block numbers and she rang from different numbers. She only stopped when our solicitor wrote a letter threatening an injunction.'

As you can imagine, each fresh contact – some of which in the early stages were not reported – sent Graham's wife back into intensive questioning. 'My wife wanted to know why she was hanging on so strongly. Surely I must have given her reasons to cling. What had I told her during the affair? Did I really love her? Was I still encouraging her?'

Meanwhile, Graham kept sliding back down into shock and disbelief. 'I didn't think I was that sort of guy, but I kept having to face that I had lied and deceived two women. I had all these images of myself as a principled man but I kept being reminded I had turned into the sort of man I despised: a sleazebag.'

Fortunately, if you follow the positive strategies for helping your partner – outlined in the previous chapter – climbing back up the ladder is easier, the second, third or fourth time.

The main danger is not slipping back but getting stuck on the recovery ladder – most commonly clinging to attempted normality and refusing to face the bodies that come to the surface.

I hope the ladder will inspire you. When it seems you have taken two steps backwards, you can tell yourself it is a temporary setback. Instead of looking for shortcuts, because they are an illusion, roll up your sleeves and do the work. When the going gets hard, remind yourself: *there is a better future ahead.*

EXERCISE: JOURNALING

I started to keep a journal over twenty years ago when my first partner was dying. I have kept one, off and on, ever since. Generally, I open it when facing hard times or trying to make sense of big changes. (I have published two volumes of memoir: *My Mourning Year* and *The Power of Dog*.) I recommend journaling to lots of my clients recovering from infidelity. So what are the advantages?

Starting to value yourself

Many people grow up in families that were not particularly interested in their feelings (unless they were happy ones) or their thoughts (unless they fitted with those of their parents or teachers). Setting aside time on a regular basis to journal says that your thoughts, feelings and what happens to you *are* important. It is the first step to beginning to value yourself – rather than receiving validation from other people (for example, your affair partner, or being devastated when your partner is angry with you).

Improving self-awareness

Half the time, we are so busy getting through the day and ticking off items on our 'to do' list that we are not truly present. The rest of the time, we are caught up with worrying about the future or obsessing about the past. Journaling will allow you to step back and spot any destructive thought patterns and behaviours.

Increasing clarity of thinking

Writing down what's going on in your head will provide time to reflect and look deeper into your thoughts. This will be particularly important as we move into the next part of the book.

Improving the ability to communicate with others

When you've got your own thoughts straight, it's much easier to communicate them to other people. How can your partner understand when you have only half understood or half formed the thought yourself?

Developing self-reliance

When everything is going well, of course it's fine to offload onto your partner and ask him or her to help you process your feelings. But what about after infidelity? Especially if some of the material in your head could trigger fresh hurt. Of course, you could speak to friends and family but there comes a point when they begin to lose patience and, because they love you, push you into making a decision or finding a solution – even though you're still at the exploring and understanding phase. More times than not, you know what's right for you. All you need to do is listen to yourself, deeply listen; your journal will help.

Stopping yourself from losing sight of your progress

Time and again, my clients moan: 'I'm back to square one.' But they're not; they are so upset – at that moment – that they've forgotten what they have achieved. Flicking back through your journal will soon remind you: 'I have made progress' and 'I'm not doing that any more' and 'I felt so much worse before'. More times than not, you have come up against a temporary blip, not an impossible setback. I cannot stress how easy it is to catastrophise after an affair. Journaling will keep this in check.

Keeping track of your learning

When you write down the lessons learned, they go deeper into your consciousness and they are more likely to feed into your actions. A personal example: I read a great article where the journalist George Monbiot shared his thoughts on what he'd learned from his prostate cancer. However, I couldn't remember what they were – despite clocking they were profound – so I looked them up and added them to my journal: 'Imagine how much worse it could be, rather than how much better; change what you can change, accept what you can't; and do not let fear rule your life.' Because I wrote the advice down, I can also pass it on to you – because I think these wise thoughts will help on your journey, too.

Tips on keeping a journal

There is no right or wrong way to journal. You can keep notes on your phone or you could buy a notebook. Every time you start, ask yourself: What happened? How do I feel? What are my thoughts? Don't edit; just let everything pour out. Afterwards, go back and underline anything you feel is particularly profound.

///

How to cope with painful feelings

In the previous chapter, I asked you to attend to your partner's feelings – even when it was difficult. In this chapter, I have stressed the positives on the road ahead. But what if you are hurting *now*, and not just a little bit? What should you do with the fear, the shame and the guilt? What if it feels like you can't cope?

Before I explain my strategy, it is important to be aware of two fundamental truths. Firstly, life is hard. Secondly, we want joy and happiness but we also have to cope with setbacks, rejection and pain. Our solution goes to the heart of the problem. We divide our feelings into two categories: positive and negative. We want the positive ones (like joy and pleasure) to hang around and get rid of the negative (in other words, the painful ones such as anxiety or anger) as quickly as possible. Unfortunately, the three most common strategies for avoiding pain only work in the short term and often make matters worse.

➤ *We try and cover up the nasty feelings or distract ourselves with something that makes us feel better.* I call this self-medicating and we do it with sugary or fatty foods, alcohol or flirting with someone inappropriate. These strategies can easily turn from a stick to help us cope into a stick with which to beat us (and into compulsive or addictive behaviours).

➤ *We minimise or rationalise our painful feelings – 'it's not that bad' or 'I shouldn't feel this way because…'* However, this strategy pushes emotions underground and they seep out as general grumpiness or depression or explode when we lose our temper and let rip.

➤ *We run away (and completely avoid the feelings) or shut down and curl into a ball to protect ourselves.* But nothing changes and the original problem remains and will cause us pain again.

However, I have a revolutionary alternative: **facing your feelings head on.** I know this sounds difficult but I will break it down into easy steps which will be more manageable...

1. *Recognise.* When you are hurting, you can be so keen to stop the pain that you don't even recognise what it really is. I'd like you to identify the feeling and say it to yourself, or if you're alone, out loud. 'I am feeling...' It could be anger or fear but it could just as easily be sadness. As you can see these are all very different feelings and you might need to respond differently to each one. However, just recognising and saying the feeling can be soothing. It is helpful, for example, to know it is anxiety rather than panic and often the act of naming the feeling will reduce its strength by one or two notches.

2. *Accept.* When you are angry or frightened or whatever, please accept the feeling. It is OK to feel this way and there will probably be a good reason why. Unfortunately, rather than accepting the feeling, lots of people beat themselves up for having the feeling in the first place. It is like being shot by an arrow (the original adversity) and then shooting a second arrow into the wound yourself (by being angry with yourself for being anxious or upset or whatever). Just accept the feeling; it is a natural human emotion.

3. *Breathe.* Take a deep breath. Be aware of the air going in through your nostrils and your rib cage expanding, and then letting the breath out through your mouth. If you are feeling overwhelmed, count the breaths in and out. It will help you calm down a little and be ready to move on to the next stage. If at any time the pain gets too much, return to counting your breaths.

4. *Locate.* There are two ways of grounding yourself. The first is to locate where you are and what you're doing. For example: 'I am lying in my bed' or 'I am walking down the street'. There is an added bonus in that this will bring you to this particular moment – rather

than getting lost in the past or worrying about the future. The second way of grounding yourself is locating where the pain is in your body. For example: 'I have a tightness across my chest' or 'I have a sick feeling in my stomach'.

5. *Embrace.* In the same way a mother holds both a gurgling and a crying baby, I would like you to embrace your feeling. You might even try rocking yourself back and forth (or just shifting your weight from one foot to the other) as this is very calming and will prepare you for the last two stages.

6. *Look deeply.* Now you're ready to look at what caused your distress. Ask yourself: what is this pain about? How much of it is about what has just happened? How much is part of a chain of events that might go all the way back to my childhood? How much is about the future and my anxiety about what MIGHT happen?

7. *Take the insight.* When you have an insight into the problem, you can begin to think of proper solutions – rather than a quick fix. What would you like to talk to your partner about? What do you need to do differently? With insight you'll have a good idea what would help the situation and what you need to avoid.

EXERCISE: REFLECTIVE LISTENING

How good are you at listening? If you're like most of my clients, I expect that you will answer 'not bad'. However, what would happen if you had to summarise what your partner had just said – nothing more and nothing less? When my clients do it in my office, they find two things. Firstly, they hear only part of the message – and then fill in the rest with what they expect to hear. Secondly, they don't hear much because they are either mentally debunking what their partner is saying or going over what they are about to say themselves. And that's when they are on the 'best behaviour' in my office. At home, they probably don't even let their partner finish before interrupting.

If you're sharing this book with your partner, I'd like you both to read this exercise before doing it. (There is a video on my website and on YouTube called 'Reflective Listening'.) If you're doing this on your own, please use the first part of the exercise. When your relationship has improved, you can show your partner this section of the book and ask to try the exercise. Before I explain reflective listening, a couple of words of warning. Don't use the exercise in the first tense weeks after discovery – especially when you are in shock and disbelief (or have just returned there after some painful incident or fresh discovery). Not surprisingly, reflective listening works best when neither of you are overwhelmed with painful feelings. Here's how it works:

1. When your partner speaks, tell yourself: my job is to summarise.

2. If your partner is talking for a long time, put your hand in front of yourself (a bit like a policeman on traffic duty) and say: 'I am sorry to stop you but can I just check that I have heard you correctly?'

3. Summarise what you have heard. As much as possible, use the words that your partner has used. Even if they are upsetting for you – like 'cheat' or 'whoring around' or 'dirty'. (If you soften them to 'unfaithful' or 'partying' or 'unpleasant', your partner will either see it as minimising or even denying his or her feelings.) Do not editorialise as you summarise. For example: 'What you wrongly saw as....' or 'Although I beg to differ, you think that I...' (It will put your partner's back up and start an argument before you've even heard all they have to say.)

4. When you have finished summarising say: 'Is that right?'

5. Your partner will let you know if you have missed something important. When he or she has finished, summarise (or repeat back) the correction. Ask again: 'Is that right?'

6. Assuming you have summarised correctly, you are ready to use the three most powerful words after discovery. They are not 'I love you' (because your partner might not believe those any more). They are: 'Is there more?' Why are these words so powerful? You are effectively saying: 'I am interested in what you have to say' and 'I care enough to listen even if it's painful'.

7. Go back to point one and summarise what your partner has to say.

What if my partner asks a question?

Your job is still to summarise. So check you have heard the question correctly (rather than answer it). 'So you're asking: did I tell anybody beyond my brother or my best friend about my affair.' Like before, check you have heard correctly: 'Is that right?' When your partner has said, 'Yes', ask again: 'Is there more?'

Your partner will probably add an explanation or some context for the question: 'I am worried that they will have told their partners and how I will face them.' Once again summarise, check the accuracy of your summary and ask: 'Is there more?'

1. When you ask your partner: 'Is there more?' and he or she answers: 'No' or 'Not for the time being', it is your turn to talk or perhaps answer the question you have been asked, or rebut what has been said by your partner, or offer an explanation. Perhaps you want to bring up something different altogether – that's fine.

2. If your partner is working through the book too, he or she will now take over the role of summarising and go from points one to seven – until, at the question: 'Is there more?', you answer, 'No'. Even if your partner is not reading the book, by embracing reflective listening, you will be modelling good behaviour and your partner is more likely to give you a full hearing and interrupt less.

On the facing page is a diagram to summarise reflective listening.

What are the benefits?

The benefits for your partner are obvious. He or she will feel heard, you are taking him or her seriously and there is hope for the future. But what about you? Aren't you just asking for your partner to pour a bucketload of sick over your head? Of course that's a possibility, but there are clear benefits for you. The information is broken down into chunks which are easier to digest. By asking: 'Is there more?', your partner will be less likely to try and cover everything *now* – for fear that there will not be another chance. By summarising, rather than defending, you will keep calmer and be less likely to get angry and for the two of you to fall into the pointless loops which suck all the hope out of recovery.

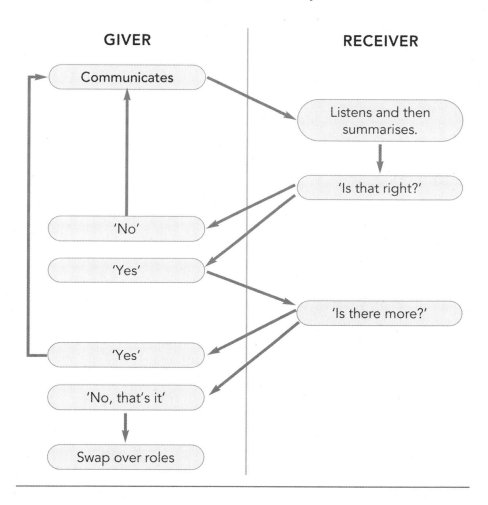

What if reflective listening causes a row?

There are two ways that reflective listening can make the situation worse rather than better. Firstly, one of you is really angry and just wants to let rip. Secondly, one of you is using this exercise as a test. For example, 'The fact that you don't want to use reflective listening shows you are not committed to recovery' or 'We're no good at this and therefore we're not good together'.

My advice is to **accept the feelings**. It is natural for your partner to be angry after discovering an affair. It is understandable that you can sometimes be angry too – with yourself, or even your partner for not listening. However, you might need to **challenge the thoughts**. For example, there is not one simple test to gauge commitment (which ebbs and flows depending on the circumstances) and there are lots of good things in your relationship which might counterbalance the fact that you haven't yet learned how to have a productive row.

CASE STUDY

Anne and Nick had been together for twenty years and both described their marriage as 'basically good'. There had been ups and downs because his work had meant they had had to relocate to different countries. When their two children were small, they had nasty rows and stand-offs that would last for days. Before coming to see me, they had had a year of marital therapy with someone else. Although Nick had aired his unhappiness about their sex life – both the frequency and the intensity – he had omitted one important fact: he had regularly hired prostitutes and had used them in a previous relationship before he met Anne.

Fortunately, Nick realised that his marriage would not improve unless he told the truth and he confessed to his infidelities. 'I wasn't getting what I wanted from the prostitutes: an intense connection,' he explained. Anne was completely blind-sided and there were several months when she swung between wanting to end the marriage – because her 'respect' for him had gone – and thinking it might be possible to save it.

During the assessment session, on the first day of the intensive therapy I offer, it became clear that although Nick had confessed rather than been found out (for which I congratulated him), he had not taken the truth drug (because several important new facts emerged as I took down the history of his infidelity). When I checked back at the beginning of the second day, they'd had a difficult discussion after the new revelations but it had not descended into destructiveness. So what had each of them done differently?

'I accepted that Anne would be angry,' said Nick. 'It's only natural when I let things out in dribs and drabs.'

'If I was awarding gold stars, you'd get one for that,' I told him.

'Secondly, I didn't get defensive and try to shut down the conversation. I tried to answer her questions – even though it was hard to remember all the details.'

'Another gold star,' I laughed.

'But I got involved in a stupid debate whether it was sex with a prostitute when on another occasion I took one of these women out on a "date" and didn't pay for the sex.'

'How did that discussion go?'

'We both ended up getting angry.'

I turned to Anne: 'And what did you do differently?'

'Because he allowed me to be angry, I didn't get quite so angry. I was able to ask myself, do I really need to know everything about the prostitutes? So instead of storming off, I calmed down enough to agree to use reflective listening. When I felt truly heard, I felt better and I could also listen to what Nick was trying to say. Although I still don't agree with him.'

'Being calmer and truly listening. Excellent,' I told her.

///

What to do about the wobbles

There will tough moments on the road to recovery. Your partner will explode over something that you feel is trivial and you'll worry that you'll be castigated for ever. Your partner, in a moment of extreme pain, will tell you it is hopeless, you should tell the kids and get in the divorce lawyers.

If it is all over bar the shouting, what's the harm in a 'how are you doing' text to your affair partner? Not because you are really thinking of starting over but it assuages your guilt about how you treated him or her. Twenty-four hours later, the emergency is over and your partner and you are back on track — at least until the fresh contact is discovered. So how do you stop a little wobble in your commitment to recovery becoming yet another crisis?

➤ **Deal with temptation.** You will think about the other man or woman. You will come up with lots of 'what if I had…' and 'if only I hadn't…' It's a natural part of grieving for a lost relationship. *It does not mean that the two of you should be together.* Instead of making contact with the other man or woman, put the idea on hold for a while and do something else: go for a run, clean the bath or phone a friend. You will probably find the feeling will pass. If it hasn't, perhaps you need to challenge some of your thoughts that are underlying the feelings. (See the exercise in the previous chapter.)

➤ **Don't feed the feelings.** It is normal to still have feelings for your ex. After all, you're not a machine and you don't have an off-switch. However, you can choose whether you wallow in these feelings or even make them worse – by which I mean listening to 'your song', driving past the places you used to go to together, reading books or watching TV shows about doomed love, or meeting with mutual friends in the hope of hearing news about your ex. If you have no contact and don't feed the feelings, over the next few months, they will begin to lessen in intensity and the attacks of longing will become further and further apart.

➤ **Tell yourself you can't help your affair partner's recovery.** I know you feel responsible for your affair partner's distress and grief. However, you are the last person in the world who can help with it. Any contact from you will be seen as a sign of second thoughts – even if you are expressly saying you are still leaving. It will feed your ex's love. Sure, it might make him or her calmer and able to cope for the next ten minutes, but at what cost? Your partner will be angry. You will be even more conflicted. Your affair partner will have a bit of hope, which will be dashed because you're unable to follow through. So tell yourself: my affair partner has family and friends who are better placed to help. If they are of no use, he or she can speak to a therapist. You are not qualified to help. You will make things worse. And any contact will be found out.

➤ **Don't go to slippery places.** This is a piece of advice from Alcoholics Anonymous. It is hard to give up drinking but it is harder if you go to places where there's going to be alcohol. A slip is more likely in a slippery place. So think about what could trigger the temptation to contact your ex. For example, don't have a drink and go on the internet (because you are more likely to do something stupid). If you're feeling overtired, tell your partner rather than getting grumpy, ending up arguing and in a fit of 'oh f**k it' contacting your ex. If you're away on business – which can't be avoided – come up with a plan of what to do when you're lonely and prone to temptation. You could even discuss it with your partner who will probably have similar worries and be pleased to talk about them openly.

➤ **Own up to your mistakes.** I will be surprised if you can follow the advice above without slipping up (or perhaps you already have). Ultimately, what will make or break your recovery is what you do about the mistakes. If you pretend to yourself that they didn't happen and if you don't disclose to your partner, you are simply bouncing around. I don't care how small you think these slips are – for example, looking at his or her Facebook page – they will be discovered. Even if your partner is hopeless with technology, he or she will crack the necessary codes or hire a professional. He or she will be able to read on your face whether you're telling the truth or simply sense something is amiss and will question you over and over again. So come clean and deal with the immediate upset because by confessing, rather than being found out, you will begin to rebuild your partner's trust.

How to deal with your partner's anger

Everyday life after the discovery of infidelity is like being on a roller coaster. Sometimes your partner is sad or in despair (incredibly low) and other times gripped by anger and full of manic energy (almost a high). Many people in your position find the sadness much easier – you can hold your partner and reassure. However, the anger is truly frightening – especially if you come from a family that didn't show emotions or had parents that fought all the time and you know from experience how destructive it can be. When, earlier in the chapter, I suggested that you accept your partner's anger, you probably thought 'Easier said than done' or 'Yes, but...' So how do you deal with your partner's anger?

Learn to differentiate the different degrees

There are many types of anger, from irritated to rage. But if you are uncomfortable with anger, you will ignore or tiptoe around the mild end of the scale – in the hope that it will go away. And sometimes in the past, it did, but what's more likely is that your partner would get increasingly angry – no matter how much you tried to mollify him or her. After an affair, it is almost inevitable that she or he will explode – as there's plenty of kindling lying around to throw onto the fire.

So returning to the idea of accepting your partner's anger... It is much easier to deal with the mild forms. If your partner seems snappy or surly, it's often a sign of muffled sorrow or pain. So look beyond his or her immediate mood, show some compassion and reassure him or her that you do care. For example, you could ask: 'Is there something about my affair that is troubling you which you'd like to talk about?' or 'I can see that you are having a hard day and I am full of remorse because it reminds me how much I have hurt you.' If you show compassion for your partner's feelings – even if they make you feel uncomfortable – you will reap the benefits.

Name the feeling

It is helpful for both you and your partner to know where you are on the scale. So name the feeling that you're witnessing – because this gives the underlying message that you *accept* their feelings. (I am sorry that I keep making the same point, but if you only take this one idea from the book, it will make a big difference to your outcome.) So how do you name the feeling? It's quite simple: observe your partner and see what feelings you have inside (because you will be able to pick up his or her mood). For example: 'I can see that you're upset...' Don't worry if you get it wrong, your partner will correct you. 'No, I am angry.' Repeat it back. 'You're angry.'

Perhaps naming the feeling will make your partner stop and reflect. 'No, I'm not upset, I'm anxious.' This information is gold dust because it is easier to deal with anxiety than anger.

To help you think about the degrees of anger, I have put together an anger thermometer but it is important to stress that these are my gradients and everyone will have a different scale.

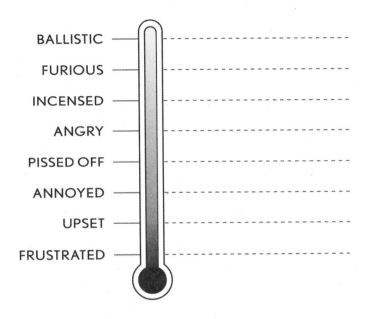

BALLISTIC

FURIOUS

INCENSED

ANGRY

PISSED OFF

ANNOYED

UPSET

FRUSTRATED

Don't try and manage it

It is not your job to manage your partner's feelings – even though you love and want the best for him or her. I know all the popular love songs tell you to be 'the wind beneath my wings' or 'you raise me up', but these are just nice romantic ideas rather than recipes for a good relationship.

If you find this idea hard to accept, look back to your childhood. Did you feel responsible for one or other of your parents? Perhaps one of them was cruel or an alcoholic or dismissive of the other and you tried to alleviate the pain? Could you still be responding to old scripts that are no longer appropriate?

If you are still rebelling against this idea, look at what happens when you try and manage your partner's anger. My guess is that it just makes him or her angrier. In effect, you are trying to manage the anger by rationalising it into something smaller ('It's not that bad' or 'You've got it wrong') and therefore making it easier to solve. In your partner's head, this will come across as being dismissive.

Listen

Although it's not your job to manage your partner's anger, you can help (rather than walking away and thereby dismissing his or her feelings). *You can listen.* I cannot emphasise how important this will be to your partner's recovery. By listening, you are sending the message: 'I care about your feelings.' And even more importantly: 'I will still be here even if you are not showing your best side.'

I am not asking for you to come up with a solution to your partner's anger. I am just asking you to listen and, if you are feeling strong enough, to reflect back some of the key points. (See the exercise on page 86 earlier in the chapter.)

Stay in the crucible of conflict

I would not be surprised if you would rather avoid a row. Angry people don't make pleasant companions. However, time and again, I have seen in my therapy room that if couples stay with the anger – what I call staying in the 'crucible of conflict' – for a bit longer, then they reach a calmer place. At this point, they will begin to discuss the issues and get a clearer understanding of each other's viewpoints and maybe even make some progress towards a solution.

Next time your partner is angry and you're feeling overwhelmed, remind yourself that anger – properly expressed – will burn itself out. Stay in the crucible of conflict for even a few minutes longer than normal and you will discover an important truth: resentment can last for ever, but anger will pass.

Accept your own anger

Most of my clients who seem too anxious to police their partner's anger turn out to be angry themselves. I don't often quote the Bible but this one reveals an important human truth: 'Why do you look at the speck in your brother's eye, but do not consider the plank in your own eye?' Sure, you might not be shouting or directly expressing your anger but it could be leaking out in sarcastic comments, general coldness or nitpicking. These will all become fuel to your partner's anger.

So if I'm asking you to accept your partner's anger, it is only fair that I ask you to accept your own. This doesn't mean matching criticism with more criticism or shouting louder. I would ask you to REPORT your feelings. For example: 'I am angry' or 'I am frustrated' or 'I am overwhelmed'.

Reassure

Time and again, I discover that under anger is normally fear. So when you have listened to your partner's anger – without trying to 'manage' it or 'solve' the underlying problem – you can begin to address your partner's anxieties. He or she is worried that your relationship is past repair, you won't get to the bottom of what caused the affair and that you might be tempted again (and your partner can't risk going through all this pain again). What your partner is most probably looking for is reassurance. So how do you do this? You tell your partner that you love him or her. You could express again your sorrow for hurting him or her and apologise. However, as you have already discovered, these only have a limited impact. In the next section, I will explain another way to offer reassurance.

Commit to the journey

Expressing love, apologising and understanding the impact of your behaviour on your partner will go a long way towards helping him or her cope with the fallout from your betrayal. However, it will not quieten the voice in his or her head which says, 'But loving me didn't stop you from cheating on me' or 'It's easy to apologise but do you really mean it?' You can go some way to combating this voice and increasing the power of your reassurance by committing to the journey of recovery.

In other words, you are committed to understanding why you cheated, learning what you need to change (both personally and in your relationship), and forging a new and improved relationship. Although expressing commitment to a better future is helpful, it is even more powerful if you back up the words with actions.

Get help

Reading this book is a great start. You can increase the impact by marking up sections that have particularly spoken to you and discussing them with your partner. It shows that you are not only reading but taking in the points raised.

I would also suggest going for couples counselling and considering individual therapy. (The former will help with your communication and staying in the crucible of conflict for longer. The latter will provide a space for you to explore why you were unfaithful without constantly worrying about upsetting your partner.) If you belong to a church, you could speak to your minister. Look into courses that might be helpful, too.

Whatever your choice, it is important that *you* lead the project. Find a therapist yourself and book the appointment (rather than expecting your partner to do the work). If you have decided on couples counselling, at the initial assessment don't fall into the trap of conditional commitment. By which I mean: 'I am up for couples counselling if my partner thinks it will help' or 'I will commit if my partner will commit' or 'I will do it if the therapist thinks there is hope.'

Your partner is looking for you to take the lead. In his or her mind, he or she has been fighting for this relationship for years (while you have undermined it). He or she is tired from carrying the load. So you need to have a clear and total commitment: 'I am committed to the journey, no matter what... through the good times and the tough ones.'

Acts of repair

You will have a clear idea of what has hurt your partner the most about your affair – because he or she will have told you (probably over and over again). So how could you combat that pain? If your partner feels taken for granted, how could you cherish him or her? Examples include loving texts and messages or buying small gifts. If your partner is angry about the time stolen from your marriage and the attention lavished on your affair partner, you could have more nights out together or book a weekend away. If your partner is worried about the impact on your children, how could you repair your relationship with each child – as they will have been impacted differently? (I will cover this in depth in Chapter Eight.) Think about what your partner has always asked for beforehand, but you have always had excuses not to do. Now would be a great time to put your partner's needs first.

If you are in doubt about what would help your partner believe you are serious about committing to a new, better marriage, ask him or her. If the answer is something that would be really hard – for example, giving up a much-loved hobby – don't promise anything you can't truly deliver. Instead, while you're at this difficult stage in your journey of recovery, cut back drastically on the time devoted to your hobby.

Don't suppress

Please don't suppress your feelings – even the ones that you don't like. They are clues about what is truly important to you. So think about what really hurts: where does your partner turn the knife? Is it that you are getting a picture of yourself you don't like: 'I'm not that guy' or 'I didn't think I was a woman who would risk everything'. What really gets you angry? For example, feeling you have no rights or that you are a 'bad' person. If you're keeping a journal, this would be a great place to think through your findings. They will be useful in the next part of the book.

In the meantime, tell your partner that you are committed to listening to rather than suppressing your feelings.

EXERCISE: UNDERSTAND YOUR PROTECTION MECHANISMS

Protection mechanisms are ways to avoid feeling vulnerable. They can become unconscious, habitual and automatic. So look through the following list and see which ones you could be using.

Getting angry: When feeling someone is insensitive, distant, unsupportive or disrespectful even in the smallest way. In this mindset, attack is the best form of defence.

Becoming detached: Spacing out when feeling overwhelmed.

Going into your head: Although it might seem like trying to figure things out – because you talk a lot – it is really hiding behind ideas. Ultimately, it is another way of being closed off.

Being a pleaser: Doing what other people want so they can't complain or be angry with you. It also includes neglecting your own needs and boundaries.

Feeling superior: Perhaps it is being more moral or spiritual than the other person; perhaps it is being 'right' and therefore needing to control your partner.

Giving up: Playing the victim: 'I can't do anything right.'

Rescuing: You feel needed and important because you are rescuing others.

Chronic complainers: Searching for and finding faults in partners and friends.

Distracted with compulsions and addictions: It could be substances like alcohol or foods or it could be behaviours such as shopping or flirting.

Once you have identified your protection mechanisms, monitor how often you use them over the next few weeks and talk to your partner about how he or she is impacted by them.

//////////////////////////////////////

SUMMARY

→ Think of recovery from an affair as a ladder with seven rungs. Every couple has setbacks and slides back down the ladder but, over time, it gets easier to climb back up again.

→ Instead of trying to avoid difficult emotions by distracting yourself, rationalising or running away, face the feelings head-on.

→ Showing your partner that you are truly committed to the journey of recovery will help reduce his or her anxiety.

LOOKING
DEEPER

CHAPTER FOUR

////////////////////////

HOW DID I CHEAT?

Since your affair has been discovered or you confessed, you have been bombarded with questions. Some of them have been reasonably straightforward, although painful to answer: who is he or she? When did you first meet? Did you talk about me? Others would have been harder, perhaps because you cannot remember fine details – for example, a list of everywhere you went, how often you had sex or what you were thinking when you sent a particular text nine months ago. However, you are also likely to be facing questions which are not only difficult to answer, but you have no idea where to begin.

The first big question is: *How did you cheat?* By which your partner normally means, what was going on in your head or how could you live with yourself while you were cheating? The second big question is: *Why did you cheat?*

Your partner wants to understand *how* you could have been unfaithful because he or she is finding it hard to square the type of person that he or she thought you were with how you have behaved. There are all sorts of supplementary questions: did I ever really know you? Who is this stranger? How could you?

Your partner wants to know *why* you cheated, because if you can't answer why, it is impossible to know what needs to change and for your partner to quieten that nagging internal voice which asks: can you trust him or her? What's to stop him or her doing the same thing all over again?

In many ways the *how* and *why* of your affair go hand in hand. However, it is vital to understand the difference. In this chapter, I am going to explain the *how* because until you answer this question, it is almost impossible to address the *why*. Unfortunately, when your partner is in a particularly dark place, he or she will probably be asking both *how* and *why* at the same time…

CASE STUDY

Here is a recent post on my website from a woman who discovered her husband's affair:

'I have struggled with how my husband could have cheated on me during his two month affair. He says he has no idea how he could kiss me goodbye with a smile on his face, and then get me completely out of his mind, so he could bring himself to meet up with his girlfriend. He said he just kissed her and put his hands on certain parts of her body. He tells me they never had sex and he supposedly met her three times and he says it means nothing. He says he loves me and that I have been better to him than anyone else in his life. So when I ask him why did he cheat he says he has no idea. When I ask if I was the best thing and I have been better to you than any other woman, why would you jeopardise us… he looks at me blankly. If it meant nothing to you, I tell him, that's even worse. No answer is not good enough and I told him unless he finds out, I can't go on.'

My reply

It sounds like your husband is still minimising what happened. He is also trying to appease you – by bigging up his 'love' for you. Neither of these strategies will help him take a long hard look at himself and understand why he was unfaithful or how he crossed the line from acceptable into unacceptable behaviour. Try changing the question: why were you angry with me? What problems did you have in your life at this point?

//

Affair Brain

To have an affair, you have to go through a lot of small steps. For each one, your partner cannot understand how you squared the decision with yourself.

'First of all, he had to think it was OK to flirt with someone,' explained Sandra who we met in Chapter Two. 'I've had men flirt with me but I told them about my husband, my children and explained that I'm happily married and it doesn't go any further. But Mike needed to think it was all right to give his number or take her number. It was also fine to phone or text and then to meet up for coffee. There were lots more stages. Going out together. Lying to me about why he was going to be away. Phoning up and making a hotel reservation. Inviting her up to his room. At each one of those steps, didn't he think about the impact on me or our son and our daughter, or about everything he was putting at risk? When I ask him to explain how he could have done it, I never get a satisfactory answer.'

I expect you will recognise these questions and I wouldn't be at all surprised if your partner is angry or shouting when he or she asks them. Most probably, you have defended yourself (which will have made things worse), you have told your partner how much you loved him or her (which will have got an angry response) or completely shut down. I doubt you will have seriously looked at *how* you were unfaithful. If you had, you would have discovered that your brain had already been primed for the affair.

So what is Affair Brain and how does it work? A lot of the elements will be familiar – because you are probably still using some of them to defend yourself (and I covered them in Chapter Two). However, don't be too downcast. If you have started to follow my programme, you will also be familiar with some of the remedies.

Rationalisation

When your marriage is in a good place and something unpleasant or disappointing happens, you put it down to temporary circumstances. For example, when your wife or husband is not interested in sex, it is because you have a small child who has not been sleeping or pressure at work and general tiredness. You can see this event as an isolated occasion and even if it is part of a pattern, you know it is temporary and when the job is finished and your child is over the flu everything will return to normal. However, the rationalising – by which I mean the story that you tell in your head – is a positive one.

When your marriage is unhappy for a sustained period of time, or you are unhappy, it will be like a switch has gone off in your head. The problems are no longer caused by circumstances but the character or the mindset of your partner. In addition, these issues are no longer temporary but are ingrained. So in exactly the same circumstances, the husband or wife is not interested in sex because he or she 'does not like it' or 'is selfish' or 'on a power trip to withhold sex as a weapon' or 'not interested in my feelings'. Perhaps it's not a switch but a gradual realisation. However the change happened, once you start to build up a case against your partner, it is amazing how much evidence you unearth – from different elements of your life together and from right back to the start of your relationship.

Perhaps you tried to bring up, for example, the frequency of sex in your relationship. However, you either didn't have the tools to tackle the problem in a constructive manner and therefore kept quiet (and hoped for the best) or you dropped hints (perhaps in a the form of a joke) or you got angry (and your partner got defensive) or you nagged (and your partner refused to budge). Whatever the reasons, all hope of being able to sort out the problem has slowly drained out of your marriage. In your mind, the problem was not temporary; it was permanent.

In the case of Sandra and Mike, he wanted them to have an active and exciting social life. However, he liked going out drinking with his childhood friends and she did not like bars. Meanwhile, she was busy following her interests in books and literature and their shared relaxation time dwindled to nothing. Mike's negative rationalisation was that Sandra did not like his friends (whereas the truth was she did not like *some* of them) and she 'didn't want to go out' (rather than he hadn't invited her to anything that appealed to her).

Negative rationalising and hopelessness provide fertile ground for the seeds of temptation but there are other ingredients needed for Affair Brain to kick in.

Common rationalisations: 'She may love me, but she certainly doesn't like me.' 'We are too different.' 'I didn't feel part of the family and I felt I had no valid opinion.' 'I have not been in love for many years.' 'I don't think I ever loved you.' 'Our marriage is beyond repair.' 'I am so angry with you because you said that you wanted to change something, which to me sounded like you didn't want me any more and regret our life together.'

Justification

'You are the hero of your own life' is one of the most famous quotes by Joseph Campbell (1904–87) who was an American Professor of Literature. What he meant is that from where you are standing, you are right and you're the good guy. So to be able to live with yourself – and still be the hero of your life – you need to find a justification for your behaviour.

Let's stay with stories for a moment: how does John Wayne remain the hero of the movie – even though he shoots and kills people? That's easy, he has a justification. They were going to attack his woman or steal from the community. In the Wild West, there is no outside authority to call on (or they are several days away or the sheriff is corrupt) and if he does not act now, all will be lost. In this way, he can do something on which we would normally frown or that would make him the villain of the story.

So how did you look yourself in the mirror in the morning and still consider yourself a hero? You had a justification. Your partner would probably call it an excuse but in your mind – as Affair Brain begins to kick in – it became a cast-iron alibi for being unfaithful (or perhaps you needed a couple more ingredients to have full-blown Affair Brain).

If you had discussed your justification with a friend, he or she would probably have found some flaws in your logic – or challenged the negative rationalising that contributed to you being in such a dark place that it made sense to do something that went against your values – but you kept your own counsel or only talked to a friend you knew would agree and offer a free pass.

Common justifications: 'If my wife doesn't enjoy sex, there are plenty of others who do.' 'If my husband doesn't appreciate me, I will find someone who does.' 'If I'm getting my needs met outside, I can be happier inside the marriage and everybody wins.' 'I work so hard, I need something for myself.' 'My lover told me I sounded miserable and that happiness is a choice, which resonated with me.' 'I felt guilty and bad about myself and needed to feel good again, and the affection and attention felt good.' 'I didn't feel heard or understood.' 'My wife never praised me and she did.' 'He appreciated me when my husband didn't.' 'She was different and made me feel more interesting.'

Compartmentalisation

This is a common defence mechanism used to avoid the discomfort of having conflicting emotions, thoughts or beliefs. For example, you can post insulting and dismissive comments on the internet but still consider yourself kind and considerate because face-to-face you are prepared to listen patiently and debate with other people in a respectful manner. You could fiddle your taxes but consider yourself an upstanding citizen or act one way at work and a completely different way at home. In effect, compartmentalisation is putting different parts of your life into watertight boxes and believing that what happens over here has no impact over there.

When your partner asks how you could have given your lover a lift in the family car or kissed him or her passionately there, you will probably never have considered his or her feelings – not because you are a thoughtless brute but because your lover lived in one world and your husband or wife and family in another. (Perhaps that was even the appeal of the affair, a chance to escape into another life.)

Unfortunately, as you're discovering, 'affair world' and 'real world' are both part of the same world. What happens in the first, most definitely has an impact on the other. After all, you have only a limited amount of time (rather than two lives) and the more time and energy spent on your affair, the less was available to your family. Your partner might even consider money spent on your affair partner as theft from him or her.

Even after an affair is discovered, it can take time for the compartmentalisation to end. For example, Mike decided he wanted to save his marriage. He signed up for couples counselling and took Sandra away for a weekend to work on the marriage and 'have quality time together' – yet he kept in contact with his affair partner (on a secret second telephone) because he still 'had feelings for the other woman' and 'Sandra was in such a state I didn't know if we would make it.'

Naturally, his secret phone was discovered and other ways he had of maintaining contact. 'He can't see that one of the reasons why I've been so upset, have zero trust and sometimes threaten to throw in the towel is because he keeps on lying to me,' said Sandra. 'I feel like a mouse that's been offered cheese to come out of her hole and I'm starving and I really want the cheese, but every time I come out, I get stabbed.' Even with such a graphic description, Mike did not truly 'get' what his wife was saying. He promised contact had ended. (You will remember that he even took her round to the other woman's flat to show her they were together and working on the marriage.) However, he still took calls from her. Why? He was still clinging to his belief that what happened in one part of his life did not need to impact on the other – despite all the evidence.

If you are still compartmentalising, it is likely that you're using the next component of Affair Brain too.

Common compartmentalisations: 'You didn't know about it, so I didn't have to worry about you.' 'My affair made me a better husband/wife.' 'My affair does not have any impact on my children.' 'I thought I was doing this for me. And it wouldn't hurt you.' 'I led parallel lives, one didn't infringe on the other.'

Minimising

If I had a pound for everybody who'd had an affair who said 'only' in my office, I would have a second home in the Caribbean. 'She was only a friend.' 'We only kissed.' 'We only met three times.' 'I only slept with prostitutes.'

People use 'only' to cut down their offence to a more manageable size – so they can live with themselves and sometimes to get other people to look the other way. In effect, they are saying, 'Nothing important here. Please move along.'

As you have discovered, your partner is not pacified by the word 'only' or comparing yourself to a worse offender (another form of minimisation). In fact, it probably makes him or her furious – and rightly so, because minimising goes hand in hand with justifying and rationalisation to form the core of Affair Brain.

In the case of Mike, it helped him to compartmentalise – because, in his mind, his actions were minor (and therefore easier to shuffle into a separate world where they had less impact on his wife, his marriage and his children). He explained to me: 'The affair had ended. I was only talking to her' and 'I only wanted to check how she was doing' and 'I didn't initiate the calls, she would ring and leave a missed call and I would call her back.' Meanwhile, Sandra was getting more and more angry. 'You promised me no contact. If you keep on lying, how can I ever trust you?' On more than one occasion, she almost ended the marriage.

Minimising happens at every stage of the affair. In particular, right at the beginning, when you were flirting, enjoying the buzz of someone finding you attractive but convincing yourself your actions would have no consequences. Here is an example from the husband of a member of my infidelity support group: 'It started so innocent, just friendly emails nothing wrong with that, but it got out of control before I even realised.' During the affair he minimised how attracted he was to the other woman and the likelihood it would turn sexual: 'I thought I had it under control, I thought it wouldn't go that far and that I would be able to stop it, but then I couldn't so I let it happen, because I had done wrong already so the last bit didn't make a difference.'

Common minimisations: 'I only wanted her advice, because you were unhappy.' 'She made me feel good but I knew it didn't mean anything because I wasn't in love.' 'I was never going to leave you.' 'I never told her I loved her.' 'I was going to finish it sooner rather than later.'

Magical thinking

When your partner asks: 'How could you have cheated on me?' he or she imagines that there is a logical answer. Although the logic behind rationalising, justifying and minimising will feel twisted to him or her, the next element of Affair Brain has no basis in reality at all. Magical thinking is when you want to believe in something more strongly than evidence and experience justifies. A classic example is: 'I won't be found out.' I've even been involved in phone-ins in which people call and debate with me when I say 'every affair is discovered'. The caller says, 'I'm too careful or clever' or some variation on the theme and I always wonder what will happen when some friend or acquaintance hears their bragging on the radio and recognises their voice. Will they phone their husband or wife and if so how will he or she react?

In extreme cases, there can be plenty of evidence to the contrary but you cling to the belief even harder. For example, the magical thinking is 'my children are doing fine' – despite the phone calls from the school, the tears in the back of the car on access visits, and the two-minute conversation on the phone because your son or daughter is sullen, uncommunicative or downright hostile.

Although hardly any affairs turn into stable long-term relationships, magical thinking says: 'We will be the one exception to the rule.' Although, deep down, people who have affairs know that the passion of an affair won't stay at this fever pitch – because nothing ever does – they still act as if it will.

Magical thinking stops too much daylight coming in on the affair and having to look at the impact of your behaviour – not just on other people but yourself.

Common magical thinking: 'I can stop whenever I want.' 'One day when they are older the kids will understand.' 'There must be a way to keep everybody happy.' 'She won't be that upset if she discovers my affair because she doesn't really care.' 'One day, he will thank me for ending our marriage and letting us both find relationships that are better for us.' 'Nobody will get hurt.' 'I can cope with this.'

Closing down the topic

If magical thinking, compartmentalisation and minimising are not enough to keep the justifications and rationalising in play, there is one final tactic Affair Brain uses to protect itself: closing down the topic.

The first variation is to have one or two stock phrases that you trot out – for example 'but I love you' and 'I love my children' and 'I'm trying my best' – before zoning out or getting in your car and driving away.

The second variation is to go on the attack. Before the affair is discovered this can be accusing your partner of being unfaithful or making him or her question his or her sanity (for example, 'You're making this up') or simply with insults (for example, 'Don't be so stupid').

If you're using this defence mechanism, you are most probably frightened. It seems like a wave of shame or hopelessness is about to crash over you.

Common closers: 'That's it, I can't stand it any more, let's just get a divorce.' 'Can't we just move on?' 'The problem with you is that you're obsessed with the past.' 'Sometimes I think the only answer is to kill myself – not that I will.' 'I can't do anything right, so what's the point?'

Why it is important to understand how

I hope you are beginning to see how your rationalisations and justifications, combined with compartmentalisation, minimising, magical thinking and closing down the topic, allowed you to cross over the line from something acceptable (like a genuine friendship or being work colleagues) into infidelity, and how you squared with yourself that it was acceptable – or even necessary – to continue.

Unfortunately, there is a big difference between *how* and *why* you cheated. I will start to cover the why in the following chapters, but to give you a flavour of what to expect, it is because of the deeper issues – some of them conscious and others unconscious – which lie under your rationalisations and justifications. When your partner has asked *why* you were unfaithful, it is highly likely you told him or her your rationalisations and justifications, *how* you cheated, and he or she will have heard them as *blame*.

This is a typical example of what a member of my infidelity support group heard from her husband: 'He wasn't attracted to me any more and wanted someone more attractive. He could not talk to me about his interests. We had nothing in common and he needed to have these needs met.' As you can imagine, she was full of despair and I expect her husband was full of guilt or shame.

Nevertheless, it can be really helpful to your partner to understand *how* you cheated. But it is important to get everything clear in your head first, and that you explain you are not trying to blame but to show the workings of your brain. Done well, this process can be a major step forward in your shared learning and recovery. The next exercise will help with this process.

EXERCISE: MY AFFAIR BRAIN

How did you cheat? How many of the techniques outlined in this chapter have you used? What really struck home with you? I hope the previous section has given you plenty of food for thought. Use the following headings to clarify your thinking:

MY RATIONALISATIONS: This is the negative story you told yourself about your partner.

MY JUSTIFICATIONS: What story did you tell yourself that facilitated your affair?

MY MINIMISATIONS:

HOW I CLOSED DOWN DISCUSSION:

HOW I COMPARTMENTALISED:

WHAT I BELIEVE TODAY:

How to use this information

It would probably be helpful to discuss your findings with your partner but before you launch into an explanation, it is best to prepare him or her.

➤ Explain you have been thinking about your behaviour and how you allowed yourself to cheat, but warn your partner that some of your old ways of thinking will be upsetting and it could be heard as making excuses.

➤ Stress that you have started to challenge this thinking and you are committed to changing but hope explaining will help your partner to better understand your journey.

➤ Ask your partner if he or she could commit to listening without interrupting – because it is easier to take in the whole picture rather than starting to dissect a small part of it.

➤ It is likely that your partner will find how you cheated upsetting. Please listen patiently and apologise again for the pain you have caused.

➤ I believe he or she will be pleased that you have looked deeper and tried to answer his or her question about how you cheated.

➤ The final task is updating him or her on what you believe today and taking questions.

What if my partner is using some of these techniques, too?

I would not be surprised if you'll start to notice these techniques being used by your partner, your children and your work colleagues. It is not that people who are unfaithful are particularly wicked. Everybody uses one or two of these techniques – it is part of human nature. What happens during an affair is that they are employed together – what I call Affair Brain, as described earlier – to form a sealed view of the world. Sadly, in the drama of discovery and the long journey to recovery, it is possible that your partner will have negative rationalisations about *your* behaviour and justifications for his or her own behaviour (which can verge on being persecutory). He or she can also minimise your progress and efforts or close down discussions, about basically anything, by playing the trump card of your affair. I will cover how to deal with scenarios like this in Chapter Seven.

In the meantime, my advice would be to recognise when your partner uses these techniques and to be patient with him or her (after all, you know from experience how easily it is to fall into these traps). However, instead of trying to correct your partner's behaviour, prompting a fight you won't win, I would concentrate on sorting out your own failings.

How to combat Affair Brain

When an affair is discovered, the walls between the different compartments begin to fall down. It is harder to minimise the impact of your affair when your partner is weeping, shouting or so distraught he or she is vomiting into the toilet.

Although your magical thinking will be shaken by the daylight of discovery, it is still possible to cling onto the remnants. For example, I've had people telling me: 'I know the odds are against my lover and I working out, but I have to give it a try.'

During recovery, when you are stressed or overwhelmed with shame, the temptation to close down the topic will still be strong. Although this is completely understandable – who wants to be constantly reminded of their mistakes? – it will slow down your learning and increase the chances of getting stuck in attempted normality.

However, from all the elements of Affair Brain, rationalisations and justifications take the longest to fall away. So why should this be? And if you have big decisions to make, how can you make them with a clear head rather than one confused by Affair Brain?

Accept the feelings

You won't be surprised by the first remedy because I have covered it before. I am really interested in your feelings. They provide clues about what is important to you and where the underlying problems might be lurking. So the last thing I want is for you to close them down. So, please, accept your feelings. By which I mean name them, look at where they are sitting in your body and truly own them.

However, I would not be surprised if you find this idea really uncomfortable. Perhaps you are remembering recent events when, for example, you got angry, let rip and hurt your partner. Perhaps it goes right back to your childhood where your parents only accepted your happy or positive feelings and you were ostracised for expressing anything else. So let me explain why it is so important to accept your feelings and then I will address your concerns.

Underneath your rationalisations and justifications, there is probably going to be a valid concern or a real problem. For example, there

117

is still a problem about the frequency of sex or how often you go out together. No wonder the negative story about your partner is so hard to shift! No wonder your justifications are still so tempting! The original problem is alive and well.

However, when you accept your feelings, for example of injustice, you spot where the sore points are. If you get angry about something, it is probably because it is important to you. I believe that *feelings are clues about how to act* and we'll need these clues when we look at why you had your affair.

So what about your concerns regarding accepting your feelings? First of all, does it help to get annoyed with yourself for expressing an emotion? I doubt it. As I have explained before, it is a bit like shooting an arrow into the original wound. Second, if you do push the feeling away it seldom disappears; more likely it will grow and grow until you explode. It's what I call 'bottle and blow'. I am not asking you to wallow in your feelings but to witness them and hold them lightly. If possible, I would rather you report your feelings ('I am feeling angry') rather than act them out (by which I mean slamming doors, screaming a few inches from your partner's face or storming out).

Challenge the thoughts

One of the most important ideas in this book – which I will return to again and again – is to accept the feelings and challenge the thoughts. Let me explain why. Along with the feelings there will be all sorts of rationalisations and justifications. Write down these thoughts and when they are down on paper, and you have a little distance from them, begin to challenge them.

Here is an example from my infidelity support group, where a wife was told by her husband: 'You weren't a risk-taker like me.' If I had this man in the room I would ask the following questions:

➤ What is the evidence for this claim?

➤ What areas of your life together were you drawing on?

➤ Have you taken an example from one area of your marriage and made it about every element of your relationship?

➤ In what parts of your life do you take risks?

➤ Are there some parts of your life where you would not take risks?

We would probably discover there were one or at the most two areas on which he and his wife disagreed. So the original catastrophic diagnosis ('You weren't a risk-taker like me') becomes something more manageable. For example, 'We did not agree on whether it was a good idea to buy that holiday home or not' or 'We had different opinions on whether to buy our son a motorcycle.'

I would also challenge what a marriage of two risk-takers would be like. Is it possible that a risk-taker and a more cautious person could make a good team? Perhaps the risk-taker could prevent the comfort zone of the cautious partner from becoming a rut? Perhaps the cautious partner could keep the risk-taker from having a disaster?

When you are challenging your thoughts, look out for words like 'never' or 'always'. These are exaggerations. Question words like 'must' and 'should'. Who says this? Your mother? The Pope? All 'right-thinking' people?

Be curious

Affair Brain is about closing down and shutting out questioning voices. Therefore, I would like to encourage the opposite. Curiosity involves opening up and asking difficult questions. It is an attribute which will be really useful in the next two chapters.

The good news is by getting this far in the book, you have already begun. I would like you to challenge yourself and find ideas from outside your comfort zone. If you haven't explored philosophy try *Philosophy for Life: And Other Dangerous Situations* by Jules Evans. If you have not considered spiritual questions try *Why Buddhism is True: The Science and Philosophy of Meditation and Enlightenment* by Robert Wright. If you want to know more about my world, I would recommend the books of the Jungian analyst James Hollis – more about him in a moment.

Alternatively, you could tackle the issues at an angle, rather than directly, by reading first-hand testimonies which are not about infidelity but tell us something important about being human. I would recommend *Touching the Void* by Joe Simpson. It is a real-life story about climbing in the Andes. In a freak storm, Simpson's companion comes to the terrible conclusion that he should cut the rope, because he thinks Simpson is dead, and try to struggle back to base camp alone. Fortunately, Simpson is still alive and survives to tell the story. The book will tell you a lot about psychological trauma, overcoming obstacles, and is a testament to deep friendship. Ultimately, it is an uplifting and unforgettable read.

You'll find a selection of other books that I recommend in the appendix at the back of the book.

Believe in yourself

At the beginning of the chapter, I explained that for Affair Brain to set in there were two preconditions: ingrained unhappiness and general hopelessness. It's the latter that I want to examine next.

Hopelessness sets in when you believe you don't have the knowledge, the skills or the courage to face a particular problem. Let's look at the minimisation and the justification which a husband gave to one of the wives in my infidelity support group; she reports him saying about his mistress: 'He didn't love her, she manipulated him. She was the only one on his side, she wouldn't let him go.' How does he look? I think we can agree on weak.

It might be tempting to get someone else to sort out your life, but ultimately, the person who knows what's best for you is you. It takes courage to say no – rather than be manipulated. What would happen if you believed in yourself more? What could you achieve?

Combat fear and sloth

In his book, *Living an Examined Life*, the Jungian analyst James Hollis explains that our greatest problem is not that we don't have the answers but that we fail to apply them. Every morning, he says, we are greeted by the evil twins that destroy our soul: Fear and Sloth. Hollis quotes the Roman philosopher and Emperor Marcus Aurelius (AD 121–180) who could have enjoyed the trapping and comforts of his position but spent most of his life on battlefields fighting the Huns:

'At day's first light have in readiness, against disinclination to leave your bed, the thought that "I am rising for the work of man." Must I grumble at setting out to do what I was born for, and for the sake of which I have been brought into the world? Is this the purpose of my creation, to lie here under the blankets and keep myself warm? "Ah, but it is a great deal more pleasant!" Was it for pleasure, then, that you were born, and not for work, not for effort?'

When I find myself taking the easy way out and slipping back into old ways, I imagine Fear and Sloth jumping up and down with glee at the bottom of my bed. I tell myself, I can challenge my fear of getting it wrong; I can challenge the sloth of procrastination. I am a grown-up. I have the knowledge and the skills. I press on.

CASE STUDY

Here is a recent cry for help to my website. I would like you to spot the rationalisations, the justifications and the minimisations. How has he compartmentalised? Is there any magical thinking? Has he closed down the topic in his mind? What would you say to him?

'I have gotten myself into a difficult position. I am stuck between a woman with whom I've had a relationship of fifteen years and two kids with (but I have been unfaithful to in the past) and a very special relationship with another woman. Originally, I left to live with my lover but, after a year, things broke down. We did a lot of self-development work and managed to apparently find better ways.

Meanwhile, my wife has cleaned up her act and would like me to come back.

My lover – to whom I have an incredible connection, something out of the ordinary – has also learned from her mistakes.

I have also learned to communicate and navigate problems so much better now. What do I do?'

Right. Let's start with his rationalisations. He tells himself his marriage has a fundamental problem and that he has been unfaithful before.

There are a lot of justifications too. He has a 'very special relationship' with his lover and 'an incredible connection, something out of the ordinary'.

What about the minimisation? To start off, he talks about a woman with whom he has had a fifteen-year relationship. It is only later he acknowledges her as his wife. His children don't have ages or genders. They are just 'two kids' and seem to play no part in his decisions for the future – but that's how minimising works, you shrink a problem down to almost invisible and ignore it. Meanwhile, he is minimising the problems with his lover.

Despite the 'incredible connection', 'things broke down' 'after a year'. I would have thought this would have provided several awkward questions but he seems to have closed them down.

On to compartmentalising, I wonder if he was still keeping the options with his wife alive – otherwise why should she have 'cleaned up her act' (which is a minimisation of the work she has undertaken). I wonder how his lover would have found their continued intimate contact?

So how would I help him? I would want him to accept his feelings. There is a big problem here but I don't think it is just that he is torn between two women. As you can see, I would like to challenge some of his thoughts. I would like him to develop a curiosity about why he had been unfaithful in the past and his part in the breakdown of not one but two relationships.

Finally, I would like to help him believe if he does learn to communicate better, he will find it possible to navigate a way forward.

///

EXERCISE: MEDITATION

I expect that you are beginning to realise that there is no quick fix and the road ahead is bumpy. How do you cope with adversity along the way and reach the promised land? I would suggest meditation. It will help quieten your mind and give you a break from the continual chatter in your brain.

But where do you start? There are dozens of different styles practised across numerous religions and even within one tradition there are countless different meditations. Therefore, I've taken three common techniques that provide a general introduction and an opportunity to sample the benefits of peace and contemplation. Try them all out and see which one works best for you.

1. *Focusing on your breathing.* This meditation can be done anywhere, with your eyes open or closed. If you've decided to keep your eyes open, focus on something fixed – so you are not distracted by other people or movements. It helps if you can be sitting down with your hands in your lap and your feet firmly on the ground. Take a few moments to concentrate on your breathing and become aware of the air being drawn into your nose and then being released. Take a good lungful, hold for a second and release. If your mind starts thinking about something, concentrate on the sensation of air coming in and out of your nostrils.

   Target time: At least five minutes.

2. *Purifying.* This meditation builds on the previous one. Close your eyes and start to focus on your breathing. Once you are feeling calmer, imagine a golden ring hovering over your head. It feels warm, welcoming and wonderful. Slowly let it descend towards your head and as it passes over your forehead, the ring expands and helps relax all the worry lines. Imagine the tenseness dropping from your body as the ring travels further downwards, especially over pressure points like your jaw, neck and shoulders. Unclench your hands, feel your stomach muscles unknot and become aware of your weight on your buttocks. Next, visualise the ring passing over

123

your knees, ankles and toes. Once you are totally relaxed, return to your breathing and the air passing in and out of your nostrils. Finally, imagine that the air coming into your lungs is pure white (full of love, peace and happiness) and the air expelled from your lungs is black (full of stress and anxiety). If your mind wanders, return to your breathing and the image of your body being filled with light. This meditation is also useful if you have trouble sleeping.

Target time: At least ten minutes.

3. *Walking meditation.* This technique is best outdoors in a park, by the sea or in open countryside, but it can be done walking to the car or arriving at work. Start by standing on the spot. Be aware of the weight on the soles of your feet and the miracle of being able to balance upright. This meditation is all about having your eyes open; experiencing the wind, sun or rain on your face; the smells of nature; the sounds made by other people. Once you are truly present in the moment, set off walking normally but not too fast. Revel in the rhythm of your movement: how your arms swing by your sides, putting your heel to the ground, and your toes shifting in your shoes. Once you are aware of your body, lift your head and look around. What do you see? What do you hear? What do you smell? Try and balance awareness of your outer and inner world until the two realms become synchronised, as this will help you to become calmer and think more clearly. If your mind starts wandering, focus on the sensation of putting your heel down on first one foot and then the other.

Target time: At least fifteen minutes.

If you find it hard to meditate, don't be surprised. I have been doing it – on and off – for over twenty years and feel I am still a beginner. However, it does help me cope better with the adversity of everyday life. Be patient with yourself. Try to meditate at least six days a week. You will find it will slowly get easier. Alternatively, you might find it easier to meditate in a group or take a class on mindfulness. Look into the options where you live.

///

SUMMARY

→ When asked *why* you cheated, you probably explained *how*. Rather than helping your partner understand, it just made him or her angrier and more upset.

→ Affair Brain is a combination of rationalising, justifying, minimising, compartmentalising, magical thinking and closing down the topic.

→ The end of the affair does not necessarily clear your thinking. You need to open up, be curious, challenge your assumptions and believe in yourself.

→ Under all the twisted logic, there is probably a legitimate issue that needs to be addressed.

CHAPTER FIVE

/////////////

WHY DID I CHEAT?

Recovery is not an easy journey to make, but I hope that you are beginning to reap the rewards of your hard work. By taking the truth drug and stopping lying to your partner, you are no longer lying to yourself. By listening to your partner – without interrupting or justifying – you will have reduced his or her anxiety. Even though he or she still has good days and bad days, I hope the overall atmosphere in your house is improving.

There is another bonus from listening to your partner and accepting his or her feelings. You can offer the same courtesy to yourself. Armed with a better understanding of how you cheated and a curiosity about whether there were any legitimate complaints behind your illegitimate action, you are ready to tackle the central question: Why did I cheat? There is probably not one simple answer to this question. Most people are unfaithful for several interlocking reasons.

To truly understand why you cheated, I'm going to need two chapters. I will start with some of the conscious or semi-conscious factors. These are the ones you already know or sort of know. In the next chapter, I will look at more deeply buried – or unconscious – drivers for your infidelity.

If you're feeling anxious about what will be uncovered, let me offer a little reassurance. I don't think it is because you are a 'bad' person. Sure, you have done some bad things, but I don't think you are fundamentally or irredeemably flawed. While *how* you cheated made your partner upset or angry, I believe *why* you cheated can bring you together to tackle these problems and build a new and better marriage.

126

If you are reading this book because your partner has been unfaithful and you find the idea of 'legitimate' complaints and your partner not being 'bad' has triggered you, I am sorry. Perhaps he or she is still lying or showing only intermittent commitment to helping you heal. If that's the case, I would also like to stress, it is not your 'fault' that your partner cheated (whatever he or she might claim) and you did not 'deserve' to be treated this badly (whatever the messages from society about infidelity) and, for the record, you are not a 'bad' person either. Remember, if any of the following chapters are too painful, please turn to the emergency help section in the appendix at the back of the book for reassurance and support.

Conscious drivers for being unfaithful

Before I start, it is important to clarify two things. Firstly, I am not interested in furnishing an excuse for your infidelity but in helping you understand the underlying problems and resolve them (rather than papering over the cracks and hoping for the best). Secondly, I might have divided the drivers for infidelity into conscious and unconscious but the boundary is seldom so clear-cut.

Top of your mind

For a brief time, I used to work in market research where we would ask people to give the first thoughts that came to mind about a product or a service. It is believed to get a more truthful response than allowing time to think and come up with something more socially acceptable. So what might be at the top of your mind?

I was angry

Anger gets a bad press. No wonder nobody wants to admit to being angry. However, it is a natural human emotion and it drives our behaviour just as strongly as love. If you tell your partner you were angry with him or her, it will make sense. If you tell your partner that, during the affair, you loved him or her, it will make no sense whatsoever.

I was frightened

Hand in hand with anger, there is often fear. Once again, fear is another emotion that we would rather do without. Partly because it goes against the myth of the strong man who rolls with the punches, or the strong woman who rolls up her sleeves and sorts everything out. Mainly because fear does not feel very nice. In fact, it feels so horrible that we want it to go away as quickly as possible.

Unfortunately, life throws up all sorts of frightening events – our employers are threatening redundancies, our parents slip into dementia or children are born with a serious illness.

If you have fallen into this category, rather than dealing with problems, you have tried to ignore your fears (which worked for about five minutes) and when the pressure got too much, you reached out for something to take away the pain. In this case, it was the buzz of the attention of another man or woman and the pleasure of sex.

Admitting to being frightened will not lead to forgiveness from your partner but it will make sense. He or she has experienced fear and knows how it is possible to do stupid things that you later regret. It's certainly better than continuing to ignore your fears or covering them up with minimising or rationalising – because you know where that has got you.

I was selfish

You have probably already worked this one out. You had a problem and instead of talking to your partner, you went behind his or her back and found a solution that worked for you but destroyed his or her self-esteem and peace of mind. In fact, it is a text-book case for being selfish. However, if being angry is frowned on, being selfish is the ultimate sin (and when you were a child it would have been severely punished).

Therefore if you have recognised selfishness as one of the drivers of your affair, I expect you will have been overwhelmed by shame and wanted to 'move on' as quickly as possible. So although you might have admitted being selfish to yourself, I doubt you have told your partner. Please think about doing it. If you do, he or she will be relieved.

In the recovery books that your partner has been reading this will come under the category of 'taking responsibility for your actions'.

I was unhappy / I didn't know myself

There is a fourth top-of-the-mind driver for affairs. However, while your partner will understand (and probably accept) the first three, the fourth will instantly put his or her back up. So it will need a bit of thinking and probably refocusing before you talk about it. That's why this section has a double heading – featuring the original thought and the reframed version.

Let's start with the first half: 'I was unhappy'. This is the part that needs contemplating and careful thinking about how to communicate. I promise that 'I was unhappy' will make your partner angry and upset. So why should this be? Remember the beliefs about love which I outlined in Chapter Two? There is one in particular that comes into play: *It's our job to make our partner happy*. So instead of asking 'Why were you unhappy?' he or she will have heard blame and get angry and upset.

However, 'Why were you unhappy?' is a really good question. Time and again, when I talk to unfaithful partners, they tell a story where attraction to someone at work, being seated next to an interesting stranger on an aeroplane, or a random meeting overwhelms them with desire. Sometimes it comes like a bolt out of the blue and other times slowly and gradually. Either way, they had no idea that they were so vulnerable to temptation, or they had been able to ignore the signs that they were becoming vulnerable. However, when we discuss their marriage at this point, I get dozens of red flags (sex three or four times a year, nasty rows with name calling, feeling ignored or belittled). Sometimes, these problems have been going on for years and years and years. On many occasions, I wonder less why someone had an affair but what took them so long. Actually, I am just being facetious. I know the answer: they don't know themselves very well.

If they were a man, they were brought up to act rather than think about their feelings. They might have even been told showing feeling was a sign of weakness. If they were a woman, nobody ever asked them what they wanted. They would probably have been taught to consider other people's feelings instead.

Whatever the cause, if you don't routinely listen to your feelings (and get an early warning that a problem is brewing) or go out of your way to switch them off (by overworking, drinking or pouring all your energy into your children), you are not going to know yourself very well. You are not going to register how unhappy you are. It's going to be a complete shock when a drop of attention turns your world from black and white into technicolour.

Therefore, I think a more accurate – and less decisive – way of explaining this driver is 'I didn't know myself'. Being unhappy is often something that you retrospectively realise and use as a justification for infidelity.

Tips for talking to your partner: Whenever you try to explain to your partner the top-of-the-mind drivers behind your infidelity, I recommend starting every discussion with: 'I don't blame you'. You cannot say it too often. It will also help him or her hear what comes next.

Remember to start every sentence with 'I'. So it is 'I was angry' rather than 'You made me angry'. The first version owns the feeling and the second blames your partner. Try and avoid 'we' – for example, 'We took each other for granted' – because that can be heard as pushing some of the responsibility onto your partner. 'I took you for granted' will be more powerful.

Even if you have admitted to your partner that 'I was selfish', it would be worth telling him or her again. It is something that you can't say often enough.

Telling your partner, 'I didn't truly know myself' or 'I was frightened' needs to be followed by a commitment to change. He or she will be terrified that once the crisis of discovery is over, everything will slip back into the same old pattern and he or she will be hurt all over again. To your partner, this outcome would be unbearable.

CASE STUDY

The following letter is from a woman whose husband has tried to explain his infidelity. It is a good example of what will be heard by your partner if you don't use 'I' statements or give a consistent message. Thinking about the top-of-mind drivers for affairs, how many of them can you spot:

> 'My husband says that after six months the excitement wore off but he continued the affair for another year and a half. On one month, they had sex. On another month, they talked – mostly about her problems. Most of the time, his lover just wanted to be with her friends, partying and getting high. So why would he continue the affair if he tells me that for months he was bored? He even claims sex sucked.
>
> 'She was a co-worker and he did her job since she came to work all doped up; but he claims he didn't know at the time. My husband claims he didn't spend a dime on her and only met her on a "weed field" to have sex. However, he did show her the inside of our house once – since she wanted to see it – while I was away working and battling breast cancer and chemo. He didn't even wait till I was out of hospital to start his affair.
>
> 'I ended up with STDs and he still made excuses that it was in my head, that I was making it all up. I'm still confused and don't know what to think.
>
> One minute, he tells me it was only sex and he was a fool to think they were both in love. The next, he tells me his body was with her and his heart with me – even though he was cold and distant with me.'

I expect that you will have instantly spotted the *fear* that her husband must have felt about his wife's breast cancer. It was certainly *selfish* to be wrapped up in his own concerns and not available to support her. I suspect that he was also *angry* – maybe with fate or the universe for giving his wife cancer; perhaps there were other issues not mentioned in the letter. Finally, how well does he *know himself*? He continues with an affair that doesn't seem to provide much pleasure – if he is to be believed – for eighteen extra months. I am amazed that he didn't spot that his colleague was 'hungover' from her drug-taking. But if he was closing his eyes to his own behaviour, it is not a big step to do the same with others. In effect, if you don't know yourself, it is hard to truly know other people.

//

Falling in love

You had an affair because you met someone and fell in love with them. It is a story as old as time: eyes meet across a crowded room and you know he or she is someone special. Perhaps you didn't immediately realise it was love but as you got to know each other it blossomed and ultimately could not be denied.

Your partner will certainly understand this driver for infidelity and even if it is not the case in your particular situation, he or she might be convinced that you are hiding something. You *must* be in love. Otherwise, in his or her opinion, why would you risk everything?

For something so powerful and constantly celebrated in popular songs, books and films, it is strange that we have only a hazy idea of what love is. We struggle even to define what we mean by 'love'. We can love our mother, our children, our dog and chocolate, but these are all very different emotions. When it comes to our partners, I heard so many people saying 'I love you but I'm not in love with you' that I wrote a book about the difference between loving someone and being in love. (It was obviously needed, because I've sold over 100,000 copies and it's been translated into twenty different languages.)

But if you're going to put your affair down to love, or you're going to base your decision on whether to stay with your husband or wife or go off with your affair partner on love, shouldn't you understand it better?

Limerence

In the mid-sixties the experimental psychologist Dorothy Tennov set out to understand what happens when someone falls in love. She interviewed some 500 people in depth, and found – despite differences in age, sexuality and background – a startling similarity in how each respondent described the early days of love.

➤ Intrusive thinking (you can't stop daydreaming about your beloved).

➤ An aching in the heart when the outcome is especially uncertain.

➤ Buoyancy, as if walking on air, if there is a chance of reciprocation.

➤ An acute sensitivity to any acts or thoughts that could be interpreted favourably (she wore that dress because she knows I like it; he hung back after the meeting so he could talk to me).

➤ A total inability to be interested in more than one person at a time.

➤ A fear of rejection and unsettling shyness in the presence of the beloved.

➤ All other concerns fall into the background. (As a respondent told her: 'Problems, troubles, inconveniences that normally have occupied my thoughts became unimportant.')

➤ A remarkable ability to emphasise what is truly admirable in the beloved and avoid dwelling on the negative – even to respond with a compassion for negative qualities and turn them into another positive attribute. (It doesn't matter that he is shy because I can enjoy bringing him out of his shell; she might have a temper but that shows how deeply she feels everything.)

➤ Despite all the potential for pain it is a 'supreme delight' and 'what makes life worth living'.

To distinguish between these overwhelming emotions and the more settled ones of a long-term couple, who are only too aware of their partner's failings, Tennov coined a new term to describe this early phase of falling in love: 'limerence'.

Limerence goes through five stages:

1. **Eyes meet.** Although the sexual attraction is not necessarily immediate, there is some 'admiration' of the beloved's physical qualities.

2. **Limerence kicks in.** Someone under limerence will feel buoyant, elated and, ironically, free – not just from gravity, but emotionally

unburdened. All these beautiful feelings are attributed to the beloved's fine qualities.

3. **Limerence crystallises.** With evidence of reciprocation, either real or interpreted as such, from the beloved, someone under limerence experiences extreme pleasure, even euphoria. Tennov writes: 'Your thoughts are mainly occupied with considering and reconsidering what you may find attractive in the LO [Limerent Object], replaying events that have transpired between you and LO, and appreciating qualities in yourself. It is at this point in *West Side Story* that Maria sings "I Feel Pretty".'

4. **Obstacles occur and the degree of involvement increases.** 'You reach the stage at which the reaction is almost impossible to dislodge,' says Tennov, 'either by your own act of will or by further evidence of LO's undesirable qualities. The doubt and increased intensity of limerence undermine your former satisfaction with yourself. You acquire new clothes, change your hairstyle, and are receptive to any suggestion to increase your own desirability in LO's eyes.'

5. **Mooning about, either in a joyful or a depressed state.** (Tennov's respondents were surprisingly willing to describe themselves as depressed: 42 per cent had been severely depressed about a love affair and 17 per cent had even thought of committing suicide.) 'You prefer your fantasies to virtually any other activity,' writes Tennov, 'unless it is a) acting in ways that you believe will help you attain your limerent objective or b) actually being in the presence of LO.'

There are two problems with limerence. Firstly, it does not last for ever. At the bottom end of the scale, it stays for about six months (especially when the feelings are not fully reciprocated by the other person) to eighteen months (when it begins to tail off gradually for another eighteen months). Neuroscientists have tracked the feel-good hormone oxytocin in the brain and come to the same conclusion. Its impact has disappeared after about three years.

Secondly, the buzz of limerence – what popular culture calls the 'crazy' or 'mad' stage of love – both blinds us to the failings of the other person and exaggerates our compatibility. I had an English client whose Canadian beloved suggested: 'You should choose an ice hockey team to support.' Under the influence of limerence, she thought it was a good idea but once they had passed through the limerence stage she decided she had better things to do with her time.

Magical Other

One of the most popular stories of all time is *Cinderella*. In a nutshell, it is the myth that someone will come along who will recognise that we are special, and pull us out of our humdrum world so we can live happily ever after.

I call the person that we are waiting for the Magical Other, and seeking happy ever after Project Perpetual Happiness. Not only has Cinderella been made into a film on forty different occasions but it has been the template for basically every romantic movie, from *Gone With the Wind* to *Pretty Woman* and onwards.

The story works for men too because by being the Magical Other – and saving a woman – a man proves his masculinity and his power in the world. However, there is a clever twist. By rescuing her, at the same time he lifts himself out of his humdrum life. She reveals a whole new level of emotion and connection to him, and he suddenly realises what he has been missing. In other words, she has rescued him too.

Instead of rolling up your sleeves, addressing the real problems in your life and changing, you can just wait for the Magical Other. No wonder we love seeing this movie over and over again.

Sitting alongside the Magical Other is the myth of the soulmate. This is someone who will be on the same wavelength as us, have matching interests and values and will get us on such a deep level that all problems melt away. We don't have to resolve day-to-day difficulties because our love, our connection and being soulmates will make them magically melt away.

Under the influence of limerence, it is possible to believe that the myths are true. You have found your soulmate, your Magical Other, and all you need to achieve perpetual happiness is to be together.

However, I question whether there is such a thing as a soulmate, and the Magical Other, as I will explain in a moment, can be a trap which stops us reaching our full potential.

I love you but I'm not in love with you

When you got married, you probably thought that you had found your soulmate. Walking down the aisle, you would never have believed that one day you would be unfaithful. So how do you get from completely head over heels 'in love' to 'I love you, but', where you 'like' your partner but feel more like brother and sister or friends than lovers? The answer is that life happened.

It is impossible to live with someone without little disagreements. It might be how high or low the thermostat on the central heating should be, different opinions on the level of tidiness or cleanliness, who is going to pick up the children and how to spend the weekend. When you were in love, and you wanted to please your partner, you swallowed your upset or your disagreement. Instead of having a row and getting it all out in the open and finding a compromise, you looked the other way. In effect, in the name of the greater good of love, you switched off your upset. Pretty soon, you are switching off bigger and bigger feelings – like anger – which you have probably been brought up to believe are unacceptable. However, you cannot pick and choose which feelings you have. You end up switching off *all* your feelings – including love.

I am asked all the time: can you fall back in love? My answer is always YES. However, the solution is never very popular: have more rows. The good news is that in the aftermath of an affair, you will have had no shortage of rows! It has probably made you question whether you and your partner are 'right for each other'. However, I believe that positive things can flow from an argument.

Firstly, rows reveal the truly important issues between you – rather than the surface ones. Secondly, they create a sense of urgency: we need to sort this out. Thirdly, arguing is the reverse of switching off your feelings. Have you heard of Pandora's box? It is a Greek myth. Pandora was given a jar which contained sickness, death and all the unspecified bad things in the world. Curious, she opened the jar and released all the furies. What most people don't know is that the last thing out of the box was hope.

So why am I telling you this story? It's because your affair has opened the box and, naturally, it has released all the pent-up negatives in your relationship (which have been suppressed, stuffed into the box and locked tight). All the anger and bitterness and negativity has come flying out – because those are the powerful emotions – but once they are released, and free to fly away, you will find hope. What I've discovered follows next is tenderness, compassion and love.

Tips for talking to your partner: I would not be surprised if you have already talked to your partner about love. If you have told him or her that you fell in love with your affair partner but are now questioning it, a good way to explain – which has resonated with people in my affair recovery group – is 'I loved how the affair partner made me feel rather than him or her.'

If you have told your partner 'I love you but I'm not in love with you', explain that you tried to protect your marriage by switching off your disagreeable feelings. However, you realise it was not only impossible – because they leaked out as grumpiness and sarcasm – but also harmed your love for each other. At this stage, you don't know if it is possible to get back the love. (After all, you have only my word that it's possible.) However, you are committed to recovery and hope the journey will allow you to reconnect with your lost feelings.

CASE STUDY

The following letter is from someone who has been unfaithful, believed he was 'in love' with the other woman (OW) but has started to question whether he might be better off with his wife after all.

'I met the OW at work, had feelings for her and eventually she also admitted the same. It moved to physical and we both told our partners. (We also both have two children.) It went downhill for me there. I was torn for the past year, with attempts to go back with my wife but then falling into the same pattern again. Now I have decided to live on my own and see what I really want.

'I am slowly coming to the realisation that I do not want to leave my wife for the OW. Explained this to the OW but she is very emotional about everything, and also very driven by emotions. She left her husband without trying to do anything to save the marriage or feeling any guilt over the course of just a couple of weeks.

'However, I think I still have feelings for my wife and hope that she (and I) have changed in the past year, better understand ourselves and what was wrong. At the same time, I also still think that this OW is much closer to a 'soulmate' – or at least a more compatible partner. It is hard to let go and I'm being eaten up by wondering "what-if".

'Despite everything, my wife still wants to try again. I miss my kids and that "peace" feeling and not running around all the time.

'I've thought out everything, haven't I? Just need to do it…'

My reply

It sounds like the fog is beginning to clear and you're thinking everything through rather than bouncing from one crisis to the next. I have just one thing to point out… Look at how the OW left her husband. She switched off and walked away without any guilt – even though he was the father of her children. As history is a good way of being a predictor of what-ifs, let me give you one. What if she realises that you are not the ONE and not her SOULMATE? She will walk away again, with hardly a backward glance, with another man she meets and for whom she has 'feelings'. Guess what? You will be just dust in the road.

If you think she is more compatible, ask yourself: why? What do you need from a relationship? When you've got the answer to that question, I've another one: how could I stand up for myself more and ask for what I need?

I know these are tough questions but it is better to answer them than expect a soulmate to come along and magically solve everything for you. It is much better to really get to know yourself, to have a relationship with a real person (rather than the fantasy perfect lover) and to discover all the subtle and fulfilling shades of love (rather than keep chasing the buzz of falling in love).

Midlife Crisis

The term 'midlife crisis' was coined by the Canadian psychoanalyst Elliott Jaques (1927–2003) in the mid-sixties, but right from the beginning there has been controversy about whether it exists or not. People can't agree on what constitutes a midlife crisis and the symptoms could occur at any age. I have read articles about the quarter-life crisis (around twenty-five) and I've had clients at sixty-something dealing with the same issues.

Worse still, the midlife crisis has been treated as a joke. People will post a picture of themselves on Twitter sitting on a new motorbike or after getting a first tattoo with the hashtag: #midlifecrisis. However, there is nothing about your situation that is funny and jokes belittle the strong emotions that have been brought to the surface by your affair.

Therefore, I would not be at all surprised if you have already begun to discount this as one of the reasons for why you were unfaithful – but please keep an open mind. Let's start by looking at a list of some of the main 'symptoms' that are associated with a midlife crisis:

➤ Discontent or boredom with a life (including people and things) that provided fulfilment beforehand. It is common to ask: 'Is that all there is?'

➤ Feeling restless and wanting to do something completely different.

➤ Questioning decisions made years earlier and the meaning of life.

➤ Confusion about who you are or where your life is going.

➤ Irritability, unexpected anger.

➤ Persistent sadness.

➤ Increased use of alcohol, drugs, food, or other compulsions.

➤ Greatly decreased or increased sexual desire.

➤ Sexual affairs, especially with someone younger.

➤ Fretting about status and the point reached in your career.

Popular misunderstandings

Many husbands and wives have come into my office wondering if their partner's affair is down to a midlife crisis but despite thirty-plus years as a therapist I've only had a handful of people arrive and ask me: 'Am I having a midlife crisis?' So why could this 'diagnosis' be popular with your partner but likely to put your back up?

There is a popular misunderstanding about the midlife crisis that is ALL about a fear of ageing (while in reality this is only a small and minor part). It is seen as a desire to avoid all responsibility, retreat to a second childhood and sometimes as a fear of death. As one client, in a fit of temper, said to her husband: 'We're all going to die one day, get used to it.' Underlying her outburst was a hope that once her husband had been 'cured', that 'normal service' in her marriage could be resumed and everyone would live happily ever after. I welcome anger in my counselling room because it brings unspoken assumptions out into the open where they can be properly discussed. So although it proved to be a difficult session for her husband, it cleared the air and we could look at what might *really* have been going on in their marriage.

Important issues to address

I am quite happy to admit that I went through a midlife crisis. It was prompted by losing a job I loved and the death of my partner (when I was thirty-seven) and took a long time to resolve – perhaps as much as twenty years. Looking back, I had perhaps five years of 'crisis' (where life was tough) but the majority of the time was spent learning and growing. (If you are interested in reading more about my experiences, I have a series of memoirs – more details of all my books in the back of this one.)

I don't like the term midlife crisis because of the baggage it brings and because it doesn't tell the whole story. That's why I called my book on the topic *It's not a midlife crisis, it's an opportunity*. It describes the life stage called the 'Middle Passage' between being a provisional adult (in our twenties and thirties) and a full adult (which we reach if we meet the challenges of our forties and fifties).

So how do you successfully navigate your forties and fifties and what makes the middle passage so treacherous? At first sight, the solution seems relatively straightforward. You need to answer three questions. However, these are really difficult questions and the answers have wide-reaching implications. So what are they?

➤ Who am I?

➤ What gives my life meaning?

➤ What are my values? (As opposed to my parents, society, the church or all 'right-thinking' people...)

These are not only important questions in your forties and fifties. As I explained earlier, an existential crisis can strike at any age. However, they are particularly pertinent at the midlife point. You have enough experience to discover that what were sold as absolute truths (for example 'hard work will be rewarded' and 'good things happen to good people' and 'you'll fall in love and live happily ever after' and 'success will bring happiness') are in fact only partial truths. There is a dawning realisation that if we are not immortal then we should live OUR life – not the one expressly laid out by our parents, or the one we chose to make them proud and love us.

Unfortunately, these are not questions that can be answered in a weekend workshop or by reading one book. Meanwhile, our society has lots of negative messages about 'navel-gazing'. Our culture is full of fun distractions: celebrities on red carpets, the latest must-see TV show, and Facebook notifications about your friends posting selfies in front of the Eiffel Tower. Your boss has sent an email reminding you about an urgent project. Your daughter wants help with her homework. Your partner is angry because you forgot to pick up more milk.

So you either ignore the quiet voice that says something is not right, you double down and work harder at your old life plan (hoping that will right the problem) or you close your eyes and hope everything will be better (after the summer holidays, when you get a promotion or your son goes off to college).

What happens if the signs are ignored?

Problems don't go away – just because we close our eyes and wish that they would disappear. They grow and grow and infect all of our life. We become resentful and grumpy. We are not easy to live with and our partner pulls up his or her drawbridge. Our brains hate a vacuum, so instead of answering the difficult questions about how to make our life more meaningful, we answer an easy one: do I fancy my new work colleague?

When our life seems stuck and we have stopped thinking about why – and effectively disabled the most effective way of solving problems – we end up feeling hopeless and helpless. No wonder we are open to a magical other who will 'save' us or at the very least distract us from our internal emptiness.

As you have probably realised, it is only a temporary solution. There is only one person who can answer the important questions about who you are, what makes your life meaningful and what are your values – and that's you.

Tips for talking to your partner: Remember we live in a blame culture, and if you are not careful, your partner will hear: 'My life is meaningless and it's your fault' or 'I've been busy leading the life YOU wanted rather than what is right for me.' Even if you do think your partner has been controlling and stopped you from achieving your goals or being yourself, consider the part you played. Why have you so willingly gone along with someone else's life plan? My guess is that it started way before you met your partner: when you were a small child. How did your mother control you? How did your father get his way?

So by all means, in your private thoughts, start by 'blaming' your partner for your midlife crisis. But also think about how to frame the problems with sentences which start with 'I' rather than 'you'. For example: 'I was too ready to please' or 'I didn't stand up for what I believed in'. After all, if you are going to be a full adult – in charge of your own life – you will need to think about how *you* can change things (rather than expect others to come to the rescue or wait for someone to give you permission to do what is right for you).

It could be that talking about your midlife crisis will get your partner thinking about his or her life. It is quite possible that your crisis will have sparked a matching crisis for him or her. Perhaps your marriage is what gave his or her life meaning and he or she is having to live without the comfort blanket of the simple messages society gives about love – for example 'If you're a good husband or wife, your partner will be faithful.'

If your partner is angry, please be compassionate. You know what it is to plough through the complexities of the middle passage – where nothing seems certain any more. Listen to what he or she has to say. Don't get defensive or try to solve his or her issues. Just focus on acknowledging the feelings and taking the problems seriously. After all, your partner, just like you, has to find the answers for him or herself.

However, it is more likely that your partner will be relieved to discover that you're thinking deeply about why you were unfaithful (and that it is not all his or her 'fault'). Share your first thoughts about the three questions, why they might prove particularly challenging (considering your upbringing) and how you might explore them deeper.

Finally, congratulate yourself. You have made a great step forward, embracing a question is halfway to finding the answer and it is much better than being lost in a quagmire of half-formed thoughts and unacknowledged fears.

EXERCISE: GRATITUDE DIARY

We don't live in the moment. We are nostalgic or angry about the past. We are busy planning our glorious future. We don't stop and take in what our senses are telling us right now.

I am sitting in my office in Berlin with the sun streaming through the windows. I have just finished a cup of strong coffee and the tang is still in my throat. I am writing. It is what gives me more pleasure than anything else. Time and again, when I read back over my journal, I get the same lesson: be in the moment, savour it, the eternal now is all we truly have.

So how could you be more grounded?

➤ Buy a nice book or notepad. I am currently using one with 'Projects' on the cover.

➤ Towards the end of the day find something for which to be grateful. For example, today I bought a bar of German chocolate that reminds me of a childhood treat – except this bar is thicker and bigger. I was also grateful for the kindness of my new doctor who really seemed to care about my health, and that his receptionist complimented me on my progress in learning German.

➤ Keeping a diary will make you more conscious of small pleasures as they happen and writing them down later brings a second burst.

➤ Gratitude for the abundance that life offers will help reduce your anxiety.

➤ It will also help you live more in the moment.

///

Depression

It is natural and normal to feel depressed from time to time. Along with the feeling comes a lack of energy, we want to slow down and reflect. In fact, it is nature's way of alerting us that something is not quite right and putting us in the right state to stop, look and listen to ourselves.

Sadly, we live in a culture which tells us to power on through, get with the programme and overcome the obstacles (even if they are internal). It's a bit like ignoring the warning sign on the car dashboard that the oil is running low. After a while, the engine overheats, steam comes out of the bonnet and you're stranded on the side of the road. In effect, if you don't listen to feeling depressed, you will slip into clinical depression.

Signs that you are depressed

Doctors estimate that half of all people who are clinically depressed never seek help. In my office, I frequently have clients who will retrospectively admit to being depressed but at the time pushed off any suggestions from their partners or family with 'I'm fine' and 'I'm just stressed'. Perhaps you thought that once a project at work was completed or after your summer holidays, you would feel better. Indeed, they might have provided some relief, but over time the situation got worse and the number of signs that something was wrong increased.

Symptoms vary but you would need to have about three of the following to be diagnosed with clinical depression:

➤ Trouble concentrating, remembering details, and making decisions

➤ Fatigue

➤ Feelings of guilt, worthlessness, low self-esteem and helplessness

➤ Pessimism and hopelessness

➤ Insomnia, early-morning wakefulness or sleeping too much

➤ General irritability

➤ Restlessness

➤ Loss of interest in things once pleasurable, including sex

➤ Overeating, or appetite loss

➤ Aches, pains, headaches, or cramps that won't go away

➤ Digestive problems that don't get better, even with treatment

➤ Persistent sad, anxious, or 'empty' feelings

Self-medicating

When minimising, rationalising and ignoring the problem are no longer powerful enough, you add something else to your arsenal: self-medicating. You know that drink, work or street drugs are not the answer but they give you a temporary lift. For a couple of hours, you can blot out your problems or get so high that the world looks completely different. Perhaps you have got through the grey week by looking forward to oblivion at the weekend.

Unfortunately, you get more and more resistant to drink and drugs. You will need more to feel 'OK' again. Perhaps it is more alcohol, and more often, or adding cocaine into the mix – but what I see over and over again is an affair. There is a high from someone finding us attractive, there is a buzz when they send a flirty text, and sex is designed to get all the endorphins going. An illicit affair, flouting societies norms and risking everything sends the emotions into overdrive. Instead of life seeming empty and meaningless, it is suddenly multicoloured again. Of course, there is guilt about what you're doing, but you can medicate the pain away by sending a text to your beloved.

As I am sure you know, getting drunk normally increases your problems. The high from a street drug is replaced by a terrible low the next day (or when you finish your binge) and affairs provide only a temporary lift and make all the underlying problems a million times worse. At the same time, the original depression has not been treated and the resulting shame, self-hatred and hopelessness can drive you back for more 'feel-good' moments and turn a drinking problem, social drug use or attraction to the affair partner into an addiction.

Tips for talking to your partner: Your husband or wife will be relieved that you have admitted to being depressed, but this alone will not help them cope with his or her resentment, anger or lack of trust.

It will help if you admit the affair was a form of self-medicating – because your partner will harbour fears that the relationship was based on true love. (After all, in the early days after discovery, you could easily have given this justification for your action. If you have had problems giving up the other man or woman, your partner will have been convinced it was caused by the depth of your connection rather the seriousness of your depression.)

In order to make a real difference to your partner, you will need a plan for dealing with the depression. This could be consulting your doctor and discussing whether to take prescribed medication or showing a willingness to understand and treat depression through a talking therapy (or a combination of the two).

To inform your discussion, look at the four statements below. Does any one of them speak to you?

1. **Depression is about suppression.** You might start by switching off the socially unacceptable to undesirable emotions but you can't pick and choose. Before too long, you have removed all your feelings and are left with a feeling of flatness.

2. **Depression is about anger turned inwards.** When you suppress your feelings, they seldom disappear but pop up somewhere else. With anger, the upset can be expressed to someone else or sneak out in other ways. For example, your boss blows his top and you shout at somebody lower down the office pecking order, or you are annoyed with your kids but take it out on your partner. Most commonly, the anger turns inwards rather the outwards and becomes an internal critical voice: 'Pull yourself together' and 'Can't you do anything right' and 'I told you so'.

3. **Depression is about having fixed outcomes.** If you were pinning your hopes, for example, on the perfect holiday to make you feel better, you would be depressed when it rained and spoiled your picnic or fed up if the children bickered. However, if you decided that being together was what counts and didn't get upset when the children were difficult (and made the situation worse), you could find alternative pleasures and end up with a holiday that wasn't what you imagined but was still satisfying. However, if you hold onto a fixed outcome – we 'must' get into this exhibition – then you are at the mercy of circumstances and likely to be disappointed with yourself, other people or the world in general.

4. **Depression is being separated from your true self.** Instead of grasping the three questions of the middle passage, you have been leading the life that your parents or society or your partner has laid out for you. Lots of people aim for a happy life and become prey to the ups and downs of fortune but it is amazing what we can endure if we aim for a meaningful life. In the Holocaust, Viktor Frankl (1905–97) lost everything that he had valued. His father, mother, brother and wife died in gas ovens and Frankl lost a manuscript (his life's work) that he'd hidden under his clothes while being transferred to the

Auschwitz concentration camp. In his classic book *Man's Search for Meaning* (Penguin Random House) he explains why some prisoners gave up the will to live while others chose to survive: 'Woe to him who saw no more sense in his life, no aim, no purpose, and therefore no point in carrying on.'

Being overwhelmed

The deeper you look into why you were unfaithful, the more the different factors will seem to merge together. Depression and midlife crisis and the need to be 'rescued' by love can reinforce each other until it becomes hard to know which is the most important.

When I first started my training in the mid-eighties, my supervisor used to ask the question: 'Why now?' I still find it one of the most useful things I learned. So why did you have the affair now instead of, for example, five years ago? It is perfectly possible that all the same factors were in play. Perhaps you might think the answer to 'why now?' is: 'I met my affair partner.' But you have met lots of attractive or interesting people without feeling the need to take it further. You might have known for ages that a friend 'fancied' you, but why did you act on those feelings now?

Forms it can take

In many cases, the 'why now?' is down to some life event that has tipped the scales from depressed or stressed but coping into an existential crisis. Here is a list of examples of factors that overwhelmed my clients: the death of a parent (which has made them realise that time was running out), the loss of a job (and the robbing of self-esteem), discovering your wife was pregnant (but not feeling ready to be a father), a serious accident (which means that exercise can no longer be used to drain off feelings), or their partner getting promotion that involves lots of travel and time away from home (which has made them feel ignored and second best).

For Julian, fifty-eight, the 'why now?' was taking early retirement. 'I had worked hard all my life. I had set up a successful company – which took up a lot of energy – I had sold it and my time was finally my own.' He had planned to travel the world and spend more time with his parents, who were both elderly and needed more support. Alas, his plans hit a snag:

'I'd always arranged my weekends around Julian but the weekdays belonged to me – my interests, my friends and my activities,' explained Heidi, his wife, fifty-seven. 'I enjoy spending time with Julian, I love him. But I don't want to drop everything to follow his whims.'

Unfortunately, they had found it hard to truly talk about these issues (or any difficult topics) and all the conflict had gone underground. Their problems were compounded because, for Julian, retirement had brought up questions about his identity and what made his life meaningful. Like many men, he had been brought up to act rather than think and he didn't know himself very well. Therefore, Julian was not truly aware of how unhappy he was or how much resentment he had built up inside towards Heidi. Everything came to the surface when he was caught out going to a massage parlour which offered a 'happy ending' (the masseuse masturbating clients to ejaculation).

On its own a 'why now?' factor is probably not enough to lead to an affair, but when – as in the case of Julian and Heidi – it is combined with the other drivers in this chapter, the result is a toxic cocktail.

So what might have overwhelmed your coping mechanisms? Why now for your affair?

Tips for talking to your partner: If you put your affair down to a recent life event, it is likely that your partner will hear rationalisation or an excuse for your infidelity. So put the problem into the context of your beliefs. For example: 'I thought I should solve all my problems on my own' or 'I felt ashamed of having these feelings so I pushed them away' or 'I didn't have the tools to cope'. Finally, outline a plan for dealing with the problems thrown up by the significant life event and for preventing future challenges from overwhelming you.

EXERCISE: THE FOUR-FOLD WAY

Basque-American cultural anthropologist Angeles Arrien (1940–2014) encouraged people to slow down their conversations. I like her four-fold way because it pulls together everything needed for a productive discussion – rather than getting dragged into the same old destructive rows. I have added my own checkpoints so you can be sure that you have embraced each one.

1. *Show up (and be present)*

Truly commit to the discussion rather than trying to close it down or getting defensive. Take a few deep breaths if you are feeling anxious.

CHECK: Are you running through the forthcoming discussion in your mind? Are you coming up with counter-arguments before you have even started? If the answer is yes, imagine gently escorting your overactive thinking to one side. Focus on your breath for a few seconds more.

2. *Pay attention (to what has heart and meaning)*

During the conversation, pay attention to your senses. Not just what's happening out there (to your partner), but inside you. Think about what really touches or moves you – rather than engages with the head (and risks a debate).

CHECK: Have you truly heard your partner or is your head full of your expectations, stories and fantasies? Are you busy rehearsing your answer? To make certain you have truly paid attention, summarise what you have heard. When you have finished ask: 'Is that right?'

3. *Speak your truth (without blame or judgement)*

Does what you have to say come from deep inside you? We seldom say our truth – we edit it or don't say it all. The difficult part is communicating without judgement or blame. It helps to start a sentence in one of these ways:

I notice…

I feel…

I imagine…

I would like…

CHECK: Don't make statements about what you think your partner is feeling; ask a question. For example, 'You don't love me' will become instead 'Do you still love me?' Alternatively, turn your general diagnosis of the situation into an 'I' statement (as above). For example, 'I don't feel loved at the moment.'

4. Stay open (and unattached) to the outcome

When you insist, obsess or otherwise fix on an outcome, you are likely to become brittle, rigid and defensive. You squeeze all the creativity out of the search for a way forward. If you loosen up and go with the flow, the possibility of finding a solution that works for both of you will emerge.

CHECK: Can I stay with the pain a bit longer? The main reason you are determined to find an outcome is because conflict is difficult and makes you feel uncomfortable. However, if you can remain in the crucible of conflict for a bit longer, it provides time to work through the four-fold way. Take a few deep breaths, it will calm you down and slow down the discussion.

///

How to resolve your conscious problems

I hope this chapter has given food for thought. However, if you're feeling despair because there seems so much to address, I want to provide some reassurance. Everyone faces problems, you are not some hopeless case. In fact, to have read this far into the book and stayed engaged, you are doing really well.

Back to practicalities, I have four ideas to start to address the conscious drivers for infidelity:

Understand the difference between guilt and shame

What is the biggest factor holding back your recovery? I think it is being overwhelmed with guilt and shame. No wonder you shut down and try and move on as quickly as possible. However, it stops you hearing both your partner's and your own pain – and until that happens, you are likely to remain trapped.

When I counsel men and women who have had an affair, I experience their guilt and shame as one undifferentiated ball of pain. Staying with the metaphor, they will either duck and avoid it or when they catch it, because it is so large – like a weighted medicine ball – it winds them, knocks them backwards and they let it drop.

Although the emotions 'guilt' and 'shame' are often used interchangeably, they are different. I think understanding this difference is the first step to processing these difficult feelings.

Guilt is about action. You have done something that is wrong and you are full of regret and ashamed of your behaviour. Shame is how we feel about our whole personality and the roots go right back to our childhood – when we were made to feel that there was something fundamentally wrong with us because we were gay or lesbian or trans-gender, not as bright as our brother, not as pretty as our sister or belonged to a religious or ethnic minority who were vilified by sections of the mainstream community. Sometimes this shaming is so subtle that we can't really put our finger on it but we have a deep sense of not being good enough.

So the next time you feel overwhelmed by guilt and shame, try and put your finger on what exactly is going on. Have you been thrown a ball of guilt by your partner but because you are so full of shame you have heard it as shaming? What would happen if, for the time being, you just focused on the guilt? (I will deal with shame in the final chapter.) In other words: has your partner accused you of doing something 'bad' rather than being a 'bad' person?

Although you are feeling guilty about the whole affair, there are lots of smaller things – the constituent parts of infidelity that need to be acknowledged, talked about and put to rest. More times than not, your partner is upset about one particular incident. For example, you told him or her that you were leaving, gave a list of practical matters that would need attending to and, after fifteen minutes flat, closed down the conversation.

'I called it my Wall Street moment,' said Lori, in her mid-fifties, who had been married for nearly thirty years. 'I had been fired, told to clear my desk and before I knew it I was metaphorically out on the street with my possessions in a box. I thought being married meant something more than that.' Of course, there were other parts of the affair that were equally upsetting, but this was the one under the spotlight.

With my help, her husband, Alistair, did not get overwhelmed; rather he focused on this particular incident and made a fulsome apology. He named the behaviour he regretted, he said sorry and explained why, and finally he acknowledged the impact on his wife. 'I am sorry that I treated you like an employee, it goes against my beliefs that a marriage is a partnership and one that should not be broken lightly. It must have been horrible to be treated by someone that you loved in such a thoughtless manner.'

Stop dividing into good versus bad

It's not just someone who has had an affair who falls into this trap. I believe it is an almost universal problem. There is a belief that goes so deep that few of us are aware of it. If I'm talking personally, I was well over fifty-five before I realised how all-encompassing it is. So what is this belief? It is that we can divide the world into good and bad experiences and that if we are clever, knowledgeable, rich or beautiful enough we can clasp all the good to our breasts and cast out all the bad. When we have achieved this impossible feat, then we will be happy. I call it Project Perpetual Happiness. You will see this belief played out in the most unlikely places – a good example would be: 'If we build a wall we can keep bad people out and we will be great again.'

But aren't some experiences purely bad? At first sight this could be true. My first partner died when I was just thirty-six. I could certainly label this as bad. But during the first year of my bereavement I was asked by someone I met: what had I got out of the experience? I was shocked. I had got nothing but pain and loss, but slowly something dawned on me. I had learned a lot. Trust me, I could have done without the lessons. However, the experience opened me up, helped me cope better with difficult feelings and deepened my counselling.

Let's take something we might think of as 'good' – getting a promotion and the recognition that comes with it. Success is wonderful but there is a downside. You can find it harder to take risks. You can get trapped doing the same old things. Pleasant as success is – and believe me, I would like more of it – we learn nothing from it.

At the core, an affair is about trying to wall off the 'bad' and maximise the 'good' in your life. Self-medicating is the same. Ultimately, Project Perpetual Happiness is a waste of time and trying to cast out the 'bad' just makes everything worse. I hope it is becoming a theme of the book. It is better to face the pain because when we do, it is not as terrible as we imagine and the process helps us to grow stronger and wiser.

If you would like to explore this idea further, I recommend: *No Boundary: Eastern and Western Approaches to Personal Growth* by Ken Wilber (Shambhala).

Get more friends

How many friends do you have with whom you can talk about personal material? How many friends do you have whose judgement you trust? With luck, you will have one or two that you can tell your darkest secrets.

However, men normally have lots of mates for a beer and a laugh and few or none that they can open up to about their problems. Perhaps this is one of the reasons why so many fall into an affair after turning to a female colleague for emotional support. I wonder how many women would not have embarked on an affair if they had been able to open up to friend when they started to feel an overwhelming attraction to the other man. Unfortunately, in our culture affairs are so taboo that many people about to cross the line feel unable to confess – which throws them more into relying on their 'friend' and almost guaranteeing infidelity.

If your affair has made you realise just how isolated you are, it is time to rethink your attitude to friends and get more people watching your back. When I talk to a group of women about the issues of being a man, they cannot imagine what it is like to go through life with the messages from society: 'You need to be self-sufficient and solve your own problems' and 'It's weak to ask for help' (beyond about technical matters like the law and tax). So let me say it loud and clear: 'It is OK to get an outside eye on a problem.' Don't rely on your partner to be your only sounding board – especially as, some of the time, the issues will involve him or her.

Everyone needs friends – preferably of the same gender – on whom they can unburden themselves and, in return, listen to their problems too. In this way, we don't feel like the only person who is struggling to cope in a crazy world.

Although it is helpful to expand your overall network, the key is probably to deepen one or two of your existing friendships. So how do you do that? You could ask someone who you think is a good listener if you could talk to them about something personal – let's face it, while recovering from an affair, you will have no shortage of problems to discuss.

Before you meet up, think about what you need. It could be a listening ear. It could be someone to point out if your logic is all mixed up. Perhaps you want some practical advice. It will help your friend to have some guidelines so he or she can be as helpful as possible (and not overload you with unasked for advice). Once you have opened up, your friend will feel able to open up too and your friendship will become deeper and more rewarding.

Take the learning

Think about what you liked about yourself in the affair. How were you different? If a new relationship allowed you to experiment and discover new things about yourself, how could you bring this new knowledge out of affair-bubble world and into the real world? Perhaps the affair represented fun and excitement – how could you bring more of that into your life? Maybe the affair was about taking risks or getting a jolt of adrenaline. What hobbies or pastimes could you take up which would have a similar impact?

If you are keeping a journal, you can explore some of these ideas in your diary. If you are thinking of confessing about your affair to a friend and getting his or her support, you might like to get a second opinion on these questions too.

SUMMARY

→ There were probably several interrelated drivers for your affair which reinforced each other and created what seemed, at the time, an unbreakable momentum.

→ Although you might already know some of the reasons for your infidelity, how clearly have you communicated this understanding to your partner?

→ Guilt and shame are holding back your recovery and making it harder to talk in depth with your partner.

→ You can start to break the blockage by focusing on specific events and behaviours that trigger your guilt and apologising for them.

CHAPTER SIX

////////////

UNDERSTANDING THE PAST

Having dealt with the conscious drivers for infidelity (those you knew or sort of knew), it is time to turn to the unconscious reasons. To truly understand yourself, I need to go right back – long before you met your husband or wife. I am interested in your first-ever relationship, not your first boyfriend or girlfriend, but how you learned about relationships: from your mother and father.

When I help my clients understand their past (and how it still affects them today), they often groan: 'It was a long time ago' and 'What is the point' and 'I can't change the past'. I have a lot of sympathy for these objections and I promise I don't plan to linger here too long. The chapter is about 'understanding' the past – not trying to change it. However, in your childhood are all sorts of clues to why you might have been unfaithful. They come from a time before you can remember and that's why they are lodged in the unconscious parts of your brain.

When you were a baby, you needed your parents to do everything for you. Not just to feed, burp and change your nappy, but to help regulate your feelings. If you were lucky, when you cried they rocked and stroked you, sung to you and soothed all the problems away. The world was good and you felt good.

Unfortunately, parents are not always available. They have other children needing their attention. They might have postnatal depression or a drink problem. They might just be really tired or been having a row. For whatever reason, they did not always have the resources to calm you. On these occasions, the world was bad and you felt bad.

Obviously most parents are somewhere in the middle of this spectrum – but I hope my exaggerations have shown how strongly our first relationships with our caregivers print an attitude to the world across our brains. And as I am about to explain, it is a very short step from 'the world is good or bad' to 'I am good or bad'.

Let's take a scene you've seen many times before. A small child has just learned to walk and has started to run, but there is a slight hill and they are going faster than their legs can carry them. They fall over and burst into tears.

Hopefully, their mother or father will be a few steps behind, pick them up, soothe them and make everything better. Sometimes, however, their parent is so upset or frightened (maybe there was a busy traffic junction) that they lose their temper or they scold their child.

Maybe the parent was busy on their phone and didn't notice the child had fallen over. On these occasions, the child will have two basic options. Remember, it's not old enough to soothe itself, so it can either swallow the pain (and pretend it doesn't exist) or cry louder (and exaggerate the upset) in the hope of getting its caregiver's attention.

Watching this psychodrama, we know the most important ingredient is the state of mind of the parent (how much sleep he or she got, how pushed for time he or she might be, their personality type, etc.). However, the child's brain is not sophisticated enough to understand other people have their own agendas and their own problems. They are the centre of their world and they believe 'I am as I am treated'. So the child who is picked up thinks, 'I am lovable and worthwhile.' The child who is scolded thinks they have done something wrong. They are a bad child, or, in more extreme situations, unlovable. Perhaps their parent can't cope with strong feelings (fear, anger, etc.), so blames the child for triggering them and goes on the attack: 'Don't be so sensitive' and 'Don't make a scene'. Suddenly, the child thinks it's the problem.

The child with unpredictable parenting gets a wider range of messages, but there is a core message: 'If I behave in the right way, I might get the love and attention I need.' However, these children never quite work out which buttons to press to get the desired response – because there often is no rhyme or reason for their parents' behaviour – and they grow up to be full of anxiety and will do anything to avoid conflict.

Over thirty-plus years of counselling, I've probably heard three thousand people talk about their childhoods and I have only met a handful of people who realised, at the time, that their mother or father was the problem. Bearing in mind a child depends one hundred per cent on its parents for its survival, it is safer to say 'I am bad' than to admit you have an abusive, unreliable or inadequate parent.

CASE STUDY

'I have been in a relationship for twelve years. Two years ago, I cheated on my girlfriend for a period of about two months. I wanted to keep it a secret, and I thought I had full control over it. During this period, our relationship deteriorated, and we broke up. At that moment my girlfriend didn't know about me cheating. I didn't give her a reason for the break-up, and that left her with a huge gap, and left her with a lot of questions.

'However, my girlfriend knows me very well, after being together for so many years, and at some moment, after we broke up, she found out. At first, I was trying to deny it, and when I could not see how to hide it any longer, I confessed. This was a very devastating time for my girlfriend. And weirdly enough, not for me, as I was completely emotionless, as I was towards anything in life... except towards the girl I was cheating with.

'About a year after I cheated, we tried to work things out again. I do really love her, and I have tried to come completely clean, but looking back at me coming clean, I have never fully done this. Looking back, it looks like I was still in some protective mode, where I was trying to make things look better than they really were – as far as that is possible. This means I have willingly been lying to myself, and, even worse, also to my girlfriend. Now, two years after my infidelity, we have been working hard to make things work again, but we fell back into a crisis a couple of weeks ago. My girlfriend says that she cannot see how she can move on with me, and now has serious doubts on our future together.

'One way to make things work again is for me to come clean, and for real this time. For her, I have to disclose my answer to the WHY question. Although I do have some good ideas I believe are true (I was unhappy in life, I felt like there was a strong connection with the other girl, etc. etc.) to my girlfriend, these are all EXCUSES to the "why?", and none of them are real REASONS. I could, for example, have brought these things up with my girlfriend, and we could have talked about my problems – but I didn't.

I am really struggling to find the real reasons behind my actions, and I'm stuck. I know my girlfriend wants to hear the truth, and I want to tell her the truth… I just can't seem to find the truth in myself, even though I believe that I have opened up to myself, and stopped lying to myself.

'I have big black holes in my memory when it comes to the "why?" In addition, after these two years, my girlfriend sometimes still wants details to questions she has. I just do not have the details. No matter how honest I am to my girlfriend and myself, there seem to be crucial parts missing, which prevent me from coming clean 100 per cent, not because I don't want to, but because I can't.

'When I look at the situation I am in right now, I can't understand why I forgot so many moments from during the period I was cheating. Obviously, me cheating was a decision, and in my opinion, every decision is based on something, otherwise it can't be a decision. I know I didn't "just" cheat, but I also can't figure out what is the real reason that I cheated.

'The "gaps" in my memory are really taking their toll now, and if I won't be able to come clean, I will leave my girlfriend with a very, very tough decision: accept the fact that she will not get an answer, and continue with the relationship like nothing happened, and for the rest of our lives together have this hanging above our heads with every decision we make, OR, break up with me, still not knowing what exactly happened, and thus making that decision without having all the facts straightened out, and thus making a decision based on her filling in the gaps by herself.

'None of the options are fair, and even though I want to spend the rest of my life together with her, I want her to be able to make a decision, whichever it is, based on the real truth and a complete honest disclosure from my side.

'What do I do?'

My reply

The question 'Why did I cheat?' is a really difficult one to answer because there is no reason that will be good enough for your girlfriend (especially after all the pain she has been through). However, if you don't understand WHY, there is no reason that it won't happen again. In my experience, there are several layers to the answer to WHY.

In the first layer, we have the rationalisation and justifications for the affair: unhappiness, lust, etc. For your girlfriend, these reasons on their own will be terrifying. You will be unhappy again. You will find other women attractive again and all the promises in the world that you've learned your lessons will not be enough. I think of this first layer as being full of justifications and what helped you to sell the idea to yourself that it was 'OK' to cheat. In other words, HOW you cheated.

In the second layer, there are habits and character flaws that facilitated the affair. For example, you do not confront problems (but bury them) or you try to be in control and manipulate, or you have not been particularly self-aware, or you bury your feelings and pretend they don't exist (until there is a crisis and you're left trying to play catch-up). There are often a lot of unhelpful beliefs – for example, what she doesn't know, doesn't hurt her. I often find people who are unfaithful are people-pleasers (who say what people want to hear and then become resentful) and often end up trying to please two people at the same time! The answers which come from this second layer are more helpful – both at building bridges with your partner and helping your self-development. After all, you can learn to communicate better, understand yourself better, and faced with your flaws you can begin to change them.

Thirdly, we have the deeper stuff, which goes back to your childhood. For example, your relationship with your mother. Did she expect you to be a good child and anything beyond the perfect little boy would be unacceptable or trigger a crisis for her – so you told her what she wanted to hear (people-pleasing) or did what you wanted and hid what she wouldn't like (and learned to live a double life)? What was your relationship with your father? Did either one of your parents have an affair when you were young? Did you need to put up barriers because you thought if anyone saw the real you, they would not have loved you?

These sorts of answers will probably gain your girlfriend's sympathy and help her understand you better. To get to this level, you'll need to focus less on the particular events of the affair – for example, how often you went to a particular restaurant and what you spoke about – and more about connecting your behaviour into patterns that started long before you met her.

//

Buried drivers for affairs

Affairs are often driven by unconscious factors that manifest themselves as what seems, at the time, an uncontrollable desperation. So what are these unconscious factors and why does the rational part of your brain – which knows this is wrong and is unlikely to end well – shut down?

People-pleasing

The first two buried drivers go together – like fish and chips and bat and ball – and reinforce each other. They are people-pleasing and rebellion. I expect to find one or the other, or more likely both, in most of my clients recovering from an affair.

Small children are incredibly sensitive to atmospheres. They pick up all the unspoken messages. They have a sixth sense that focuses in on problems in the home and – because their very survival is tied into their parents' well-being – will do anything possible to make things better. Unfortunately, when we are young, we don't have a credit card or the keys to the car – so our resources are quite limited. However, we can try and lower the temperature by pleasing our parents and making them happier.

For example, Miquel, in his mid-forties, had an anxious mother who saw disaster round every corner. Growing up, when she was anxious, he would be unsettled, worried and frightened. So he would go out of his way to make her happy (so he was one less thing to worry about), reassure her and try to make everything right with the world. A typical example would be when Miquel was twelve and went away to scout camp. His mother was so worried that the only way he could calm her down was by phoning her every night from a telephone box up the road from the camp. (It was many years before mobile phones.)

'After the first night, I was the only boy in the queue to call home. The rest were Asian girls who would sit in the front row of the class with their hands up. I had to promise my mother that I would do nothing dangerous like rock climbing. I certainly didn't tell her when I went canoeing – as I know she would have been anxious about me capsizing,' he said.

While Miquel was in the queue for the phone, his friends were cooking sausages over the fire, telling ghost stories and having a good time. While they were challenging themselves in the woods, he was often forced to do the art classes in one of the huts. He was using a type of interaction to solve conflicts that I will expand on further in the next chapter. Although he would not have used these words, in effect he was saying to himself: 'My mother's needs (in this case to feel safe) are more important than mine (to be with my mates).' I call this being *passive*.

If you put others first and yourself second, it doesn't mean that you're completely selfless. You *do* hope to get your needs met but you hope that if you make others happy they will fulfil your needs. In the case of Miquel, he was saying: 'If I make my mother calm, I will feel better and the world will be good again.' There are two problems with this approach. Let's start with the deeper one: Miquel could not make the world feel safe for his mother. He was fighting a losing battle. (However, as a twelve-year-old he would not have had enough experience of the world to know that.) The more obvious problem is that if you don't tell someone your needs — for example, 'I want to go canoeing' — they don't know what they are (and therefore can't fulfil your desires). If you drop hints, these are easy to ignore or play down.

Not surprisingly, people who are passive find it hard to get their needs met. They are putting other people first and they don't speak up when there is something they desire (especially if they know it will not please their significant other). However, there is a way when they can still please and get what they want. Back to Miquel, he did not tell his mother about the canoe options (so she could not forbid it). He omitted to tell her about his plan. When she asked what he did that day, he lied. He justified it to himself that he 'deserved' a bit of fun and rationalised 'What she doesn't know won't hurt her.' It's easy to see how this behaviour and the rationalising needed to cope with being passive as a child can lay the foundation for lying to your partner and having an affair.

Worse still, Miquel grew up desperate to please — not just his mother — but everybody. He wanted his clients at the accountancy firm where he worked to like him. He worked longer and longer hours

– because he found it hard to say no and 'let other people down'. His wife came from a big family and loved to throw big family parties (with elaborate meals and lots of clearing up afterwards). He would go along with his wife's desires – because he wanted to please (even though he would have preferred to celebrate his birthday and other significant dates in the calendar with just his wife and children).

Despite setting out to please everybody, Miquel was pleasing nobody. His wife felt unsupported, his children felt ignored. He was exhausted and unhappy – which brings us to the second and companion driver for affairs…

Rebellion

When something isn't going well, the logical response is to speak up, discuss the problem and resolve it. However, if you have been trained from childhood to please you will be uncomfortable with conflict and your natural response will be to appease.

Staying with Miquel, when he was about to get married, there was some element of the reception that his mother thought was important but Miquel and his wife did not. Perhaps it was the colour of the napkins or whether a second cousin should come or not, it doesn't matter, but Miquel finally said no to her. Her response was to threaten to get out of the moving car they were in.

'She had her hand on the door. She was getting ready to jump out. I begged and pleaded. I stopped the car. I tried to calm her down. Nothing worked. Fortunately, my wife-to-be was understanding and I told myself it didn't matter,' Miquel explained. 'And in some way, it didn't because I can't remember what the dispute was about. But I will always remember her threats; she used blackmail to control me. I often wonder what would have happened if I'd said, "OK Mum, jump."'

There is only so much people-pleasing you can do before you reach the point of rebellion. Perhaps you consciously think, 'I've had enough' or 'I'm fed up with pleasing other people, they are never satisfied, so I will please myself for a change.'

At this point, you switch from being passive (my needs are not as important as yours) to *domineering* (my needs are more important than yours). It might be that you go out and, for example, buy a motorbike – even though your partner is against the idea – or make a risky investment (because you're fed up with your partner's cautious approach). In Miquel's case, he had a long-term affair and he ended up with a mistress to please too.

Rebellion is a natural part of moving on from being a child to an adult. However, some people, like Miquel, never go through this phase. When he was a teenager, he had younger siblings and he had it drummed into him that he should be a 'good example' to them. So he never really started the process of separation from his mother and even though he married and left home, he was still pleasing his mother (and used this model of behaviour for dealing with his wife too).

Another variation on this theme, which I see in my therapy office, is partial rebellion. Christopher, forty-two, had a father with a strong personality and a clear sense of what was right and wrong. He often lectured against 'wasters' – who ended up in the prison service where he worked. Naturally, his son worked hard, got good grades and was the model son. He certainly did not embarrass him by hanging out with the 'bad' boys at school who smoked behind the bicycle sheds and skipped compulsory games. When Christopher hit his teens, his relationship with his father became rocky: 'I would start to have different views on the politics of the day and the conversations round the dinner table became quite heated,' Christopher explained. 'Fortunately, I went off to university before we came to serious blows.'

It was great that he had started to stand up for himself, but only in a way that was acceptable to his father, who relished a debate (and probably thought he would grow out of his 'youthful idealism' and realise 'the errors of his ways'). However, Christopher had not challenged his father's rules and had, unwittingly, installed his father's voice in his head.

'I work crazy hours. I know it's way too much and I make all these plans to slow down but somehow they never come to anything,' he explained.

'Because if you sit down and do nothing, your conscience says don't be a waster?' I asked.

Christopher nodded sadly.

The parallels between Christopher and his father's careers were extraordinary – working all hours, both were on committees that advised the government (albeit in different fields), and speaking at conferences all over the country. The time away from home had been an issue for his mother with his father and, not surprisingly, was one between Christopher and his wife.

The Jungian analyst James Hollis believes we are born twice. The first time when we arrive in the world, and the second when we realise that we only have one life and we should follow our own path (rather than repeat our father's or mother's because that has already been done). Sadly, lots of people never lead their own path and continue to follow the rules set down by their parents (or just do the opposite, which is still giving them a central role in their lives).

If you have had a partial rebellion like Christopher – and follow your parents' rules rather than working out your own – you are likely to know deep down that something is not right. However, if you are too busy working (like Christopher) to reflect deeply, you are unlikely to realise the driver for your behaviour. Instead of becoming your own person, you rebel against the person closest: your partner. Christopher ended up having a long affair because he felt 'unsupported' at home – rather than questioning the values that had been drummed into him which were undermining his happiness, his health and his peace of mind.

Time and again, I see this fatal combination of people-pleasing followed by rebellion – best summed up in this case from my infidelity support group:

'My husband was scared of being a father, he couldn't talk to me, I had "forced" him to have a baby he wasn't ready for, etc. I was focused on our baby and not on him.'

Unresolved childhood issues

It is possible that you might know the driver for your affair but because it happened so long ago, you haven't joined the dots from your the past to today. In effect, the why of your affair has been hiding in plain view.

Here is a story posted onto my website where the wife has connected unresolved childhood issues to her husband's recent affair:

'When my husband was thirteen, his mother gave birth to two girls back to back, the second one being unplanned and unwanted. His mom was depressed and devastated. My husband's father was/ is very absent emotionally (doesn't have the tools, poor man). So at the age of thirteen, my husband engages in sexual relationships! That becomes the place for him to get the much-needed attention, love, desire. I only learned about these details when we got married. He had deliberately not shared them with me thinking I would judge him. That is why he is so insecure, thinking I would not have accepted him. Truth is, I wish he had been honest. But honesty is a characteristic that comes with self-esteem, which he lacked – even though he was extremely over-accomplished and came across as the most confident person!

'In his family, emotions are a difficult topic for people to handle. Everyone likes to put their head in the sand and pretend it will all just pass. They are "forward-looking" (running away from ever discussing difficult things).

'It was only after this affair that my husband understood "mental health matters"! Before that, vulnerability was considered a weakness. This catastrophe was extremely painful, but it was also a unique learning/growing opportunity.'

Of course not everybody who had a difficult childhood goes on to have an affair, but one of the ways of coping with pain when you are young is telling yourself that everything will be different when you grow up (and gain 'control' over your life); you are not going to make the same mistakes as your parents and you are going to find someone who will love, accept and save you. And indeed, for many years it can be just as you promised yourself. However, life has a way of throwing up challenges – like serious illness, a job loss, or your child reaching the same age as you were when your parents divorced – and the unresolved issues rise to the surface.

When the pain is too much to bear, perhaps because you have not made the connections, or because it involved abuse or trauma, you might have distracted yourself and tried to soothe yourself with the temporary 'feel good' elements of an affair.

So think back to your childhood. What happened which other people might consider tough (but perhaps your family played down)? Did one of your parents die? Was one of your siblings disabled or died young? Did your father have a financial crisis and the family had to downsize or move a lot? Did one or both of your parents have an affair (even if they subsequently stayed together)?

Whatever the circumstances, how did the changes impact you? How did you believe that you needed to behave – even if nobody gave an explicit instruction? For example: did you need to be a good child (so your parents did not have to deal with any more upset)? Did you become your mother's or father's little supporter (and grow up very quickly)? Or did you work extra hard at school (to make everybody pleased about something)?

One final question: how could these unresolved problems from the past be exacerbating the problems today?

CASE STUDY

'My husband and I have been married for ten years this year. We married for love and I don't regret it but we have faced some unique challenges. I wonder if you could help shed some light on how to move forward in the aftermath of what now feels like a midlife crisis. I am now thirty-two.

'I was born in a capital city and moved to the countryside when I married my husband. I suffered with varying levels of depression on and off over the years and at that time I had had enough and really wanted to just leave and get out of the city.

'Looking back, I was really naive and had no idea of the ways in which I could be handicapping my career or isolating myself – but I was so unhappy after ending a bad relationship abroad that I just wanted a fresh start somewhere new and completely obscure. Not sure if this was the best move, but it provided me with the space to deal with a lot of my issues through counselling.

'This had its upside and I feel I have learned a lot from being here and raising our only child (seven years old). However, over the last couple of years the remoteness and boredom of the rustic life really began to get me down, and regrettably I acted without having thought everything through.

'Our issue was further complicated by the fact that my daughter was sexually assaulted by my mother-in-law's new husband, which "blew me up as a mother", when she was just four. We (I) did the right thing and contacted the authorities, police, etc. – however, this was a harrowing experience for us and we no longer have contact with this side of the family. My own family do not live nearby and it felt hard to leave our child with anyone for a long time – which has limited our childcare options over the last few years.

'I have a few friends in the area but no one close enough to share the daily anguish this has caused over the past few years. My husband did an amazing job of putting his daughter first and I am proud of his courage as his mother no longer talks to him and has taken her partner's side.

'It feels like a disgusting shadow over our marriage for me – as ironically my sister was sexually abused as a child and I remember thinking before the conception of my daughter that with my husband (and his family) something like that could never happen with them. They seemed the picture-perfect version of middle-class success when compared to my chaotic and emotionally charged working-class upbringing. I still feel guilt and shame that I couldn't protect my child from this happening in the first place – but I (we) concentrated all our energy on making her feel secure, stable and loved during and after the initial disclosure.

'However, the abuse has really tainted my marriage for me – even though we did everything by the book and managed to somehow go on living despite the trauma. My husband works for a family company, which threw up unexpected complications about us being able to move away and be closer to my family for a fresh start.

'At the time, I felt like I was the only one who had any emotions about these issues and it was like there was an elephant in the room for me for two years or so as my husband's family don't express much. My husband is really wonderful with dealing with the practical issues like keeping house and tidying but just SHUT DOWN and carried on business as usual when it came to anything outside his routine.

'When I turned thirty, I snapped. I went away on holiday with my best friend who shares a birthday and ended up flirting and kissing one or two strangers when drunk. It was a slippery slope from there. At one point, I must have just felt like the rules didn't apply any more. It sounds terrible but I just began to question the point of anything: life didn't seem 'fair'; terrible things still happened to innocent children/families/people. I started to question the point of fidelity and marital monogamy deeply and would have open discussions with my husband about this. We tried counselling, unsuccessfully, for six weeks around the same time...

'I was feeling restless and asked for my husband's consent to see other people – and began a close relationship with a man for a few months. At the time, I felt justified but it did nothing for our marriage obviously. Later, he said he thought I would do what I wanted anyway and that's why he consented, which greatly annoyed me because he did not give me a chance to hear his true feelings at the time. I broke it off when I realised my husband was hurting. However, I became angry that he did not know himself well enough to ask me to stop – which somehow made me feel justified in my behaviour.

'Next, I arranged a separation of a few months and took my child for a holiday abroad. I was staying with a close friend and we occasionally went on drink-fuelled flings and I was unfaithful again. Although I now regret my actions, at the time, I believed I deserved to be this joyfully scandalous person. On reflection, I see how much I was hurting and how little these actions served to help the situation.

'Meanwhile my husband was suffering and lost a lot of weight. I am sad I felt my actions needed to be this drastic to get him to notice my unhappiness. He has since said how much he felt let down that I wanted to be with other men – and I wish he could have found his words much earlier.

'After risking everything just for something to "change", I am back home – at least my mindset has changed. We are trying to work things out – but I feel in my desperation that I not only compromised my marriage, but my oldest friendships too. I worry things won't change and my life will just pass by here, but my husband feels tethered to his family's company.

'My heart is heavy as I write this – but every life catastrophe so far has taught me that there is a tiny sliver of life-affirming wonder attached to any disaster…somewhere – please help me to find it.

'I am trying to learn how to go forward but the lack of clarity and the feeling that I have screwed things up so badly makes it hard sometimes to get up in the mornings. I still live in the same small village with the same bunch of people I ran away from – even though our house has been for sale for a year. I feel desperate to start again without the past following me around like a constant bad smell. I feel I have hurt people, I have hurt myself and I regret this daily.

'Where do I start to fix things?'

My reply

Thank you for your brave letter and for taking the time to understand yourself. Congratulations on supporting your daughter with the abuse so thoroughly. However, I wonder who supported and comforted you? It sounds like nobody. Worse still, it brought up all the abuse from your childhood (albeit it to your sister). It sounds like none of this has been processed properly and that in some way your 'scandalous' behaviour is connected to the abuse.

A good book for thinking about the impact of the past on today is *The Drama of Being a Child* by Alice Miller. To think about fixing yourself, have a look at my book, *Wake Up and Change Your Life*.

So what is the life-affirming sliver of hope in all this? You have learned to look before you leap. You have discovered how a quick and easy solution – like the flattery of strangers – makes everything better for a moment but a thousand times worse in the long term. Furthermore, you are committed to changing.

Sounds like more than a sliver of life-affirming wonder to me!

///

Addiction

The next driver for affairs will be hard to own up to. Although your family might have commented on your drinking, recreational drug consumption, shopping, gaming, gambling or some other behaviour, you have got angry and defensive. I am not saying that you are an addict. I don't know you. It's not my area of expertise but, having said that, I meet a lot of people who have been using something, most commonly alcohol, as a way of coping with stress or unwinding at the end of the day. However, recently it has changed from a stick to support them into a stick to beat them. In effect, they have turned from someone who uses, to someone who abuses.

The problem is partly that as you get older, your body takes longer to process, for example, the alcohol. You need to drink more to get the same response. If you have been drinking to self-medicate – for depression, anxiety or some unresolved personal problems – it is unlikely the underlying issues have eased. In fact, they are likely to have got worse and your family will be 'on your back' more – which in turn encourages more consumption to 'forget' or to 'escape'.

At this point, many people who self-medicate will add a secondary stimulant or tranquillising substance/behaviour into the mix or sometimes a third. This is the point at which they often end up in my office.

In the last three months, I've had a client who'd been banished to the garage – because his wife could not stand his drinking and smoking in the living room – who decided to pass the time in exile by flirting online and texting other women. Not surprisingly, his already compromised relationship with his wife took a turn for the worse when she discovered it was not 'harmless fun' and that he had arranged to meet several of them.

I had another client who would go out drinking two or three times a week with his mates, many of whom he had known from his school days. His consumption of alcohol was already a cause of concern for his wife – as he would sometimes look 'green' the next morning after a 'heavy session' and not be able to get out of bed on Sunday until the middle of the afternoon. However, when his behaviour became more erratic, she discovered he had been using cocaine and had had an affair with a much younger 'party girl'. While she could just about tolerate the drinking – he had been a heavy drinker when they met and she had taken the credit for 'steadying' him – she was distraught about the other woman and had taken advice about getting a divorce. Worse still, his attempts to 'save' his marriage were forever being compromised because he found it so 'hard' to give up calling or taking calls from the other woman.

'I can't stop myself,' he explained in one of our sessions, 'I resolve not to answer but she phones and I think, "I'll just see how she is, what she wants"…'

'Just the one call,' I reply.

He nods.

'Similar to just one drink and you know where that ends…' I added.

A third client had a gambling addiction which he had managed over the years because he had a good job (so he could hide the full extent of his losses) and by avoiding weekends away with his brother (who was a 'bad influence'). Once again, his wife would be angry – but ultimately forgiving – when he lost large sums of money, but 'completely in pieces' when he had a short affair with a work colleague 'who meant nothing' to him. Fortunately, by the time he reached my office, he had entered a twelve-step programme and begun to understand the origin of his gambling addictions. He was abused by a teacher at school – but had never told anyone and as a child 'managed' his pain by temporarily blocking it out with the 'excitement' of trying to win the jackpot on machines in various takeaway outlets in the small town where he grew up. When we talked more about the affair, there were strong similarities between how the teacher 'groomed' him and how the work colleague went about pursuing him. On both occasions, he disassociated from his body and watched what happened from above.

If you are concerned that drink or some other substance or behaviour has facilitated your infidelity – by reducing inhibitions and judgement – or is one of the main drivers, it is important to take a twin-track approach: working on the addiction issues *and* the marriage problems at the same time. It will give your partner extra reassurance if you seek professional help or join one of the fellowships for addicts.

Firstly, it shows you are taking the problem seriously. Secondly, you are less likely to get drunk, or into an altered state, and contact the other man or woman again.

What about love and sex addiction? Is it possible to be addicted to another person? Is sex addiction just an excuse for not being able to control your urges? While addiction to drink, prescription and street drugs have clear health implications, the objection to lots of sex is more moral (although sexually transmitted diseases are an issue with multiple partners). Could all the coverage of sex addiction be just the latest media hype and another way of the authorities telling us what to do?

Both love and sex addiction are more complex and controversial than the other forms of addiction, and for that reason, I have left these till last to discuss. Starting with love addiction, there is certainly a fellowship for people who feel addicted to romance and the high from limerence (see page 132). It could be that you've found the pull of your affair partner like an addiction (and a harder one to kick because your dealer – or your 'lover' – has kept phoning and offering another hit). However, it is equally possible that you consider comparing your love for your affair partner with the high of drink or drugs offensive. My advice is always: if you find the term helpful (and a useful way to explain the affair to your partner), that's fine. If it does not speak to you, that's fine too.

Moving on to sex addiction, I am always reminded of the joke: what is the definition of promiscuous? Answer: someone who has more sex than you! Jacob, fifty-three, would zone out with binges of pornography that would last for several hours and would use sex with prostitutes as a 'reward' for hard work and a way of 'cheering' himself up when work went badly. Worse still, he felt terrible afterwards and the way he was treating the working women was bleeding into his relationships with all women. 'My goal was to find a wife and have a family but I would find myself getting impatient and pushy if a date didn't move into the sex sphere quickly enough for my liking. I was sabotaging my goals.' When I talked about sex addiction, Jacob found the idea helpful because it allowed him to re-evaluate. He stopped both porn and prostitutes and started his longest relationship in years.

For other clients, dating several women on the internet at the same time or exploring different fetishes was about general unhappiness and a healthy curiosity rather than addiction. Certainly, there is no agreed definition of what constitutes a sex addiction and there is a debate amongst professionals about whether 'behavioural' addictions are as valid as 'chemical' ones. Some therapists only use the term because that is what their clients call their obsessive drive for sex (which never properly satiates their desire, makes their lives unmanageable and themselves utterly miserable). So, back to you... Does the term help or hinder you?

If any part of this discussion has got you thinking about addiction and you want to understand more, I have some recommended books in the appendix at the back of the book.

On the spectrum

There used to be a division between the neurodevelopmental categories of Autism and Asperger syndrome – with the second being a milder form of the first. However, more recently, experts talk about one spectrum with all of us on it. At one end of the scale are people with severe autism (who were diagnosed as children) and the other is a majority of the population who are described as 'neurologically typical'.

If you are 'on the spectrum', your brain will be wired differently from most other people's. It could be that you can hold more data in your head or see unusual and sometimes profitable connections. It is no coincidence that many of the founding fathers of the tech and social media companies are on the spectrum. Figures from history, like Michelangelo, who made great leaps forward in their respective fields, have also been subsequently diagnosed. It can also be a problem as well as an advantage. You might be particularly sensitive to noises or tastes or have synaesthesia – where with letters, shapes, numbers or people's names comes an extra sensory perception such as smell, colour or flavour. If you are on the spectrum, while your brain is busy with all this 'extra' information, you could be missing out on what everybody else takes for granted: non-verbal communication and reading other people's emotions. Unfortunately, you find it hard to read important social cues or you are considered odd, weird or dismissed as a 'nerd'. It is highly likely that your partner will complain that you lack empathy. Conversely, you will complain that other people 'don't mean what they say' and lots of their decisions are illogical.

People on the spectrum often have special interests or hobbies – where the world is ordered and rules of engagement are predictable. For example, 'Dungeons and Dragons' or motor sports or horse riding. They feel safe, can relax and unwind. However, some autistic people will have repetitive patterns – called stimming – where they rock, handclap or repeat words to feel safe. I have a client who would deal with over-stimulation by climbing into a cupboard and closing the door. One woman would hail a taxi and ask the driver to drive around for a while (until she had decompressed from the outside world). There are four times more boys than girls who are diagnosed as children as being on the spectrum. However, it is possible that our emphasis on girls being 'social' means they learn to disguise differences better than boys.

So how does an affair lead to a recognition that you might be on the spectrum? After the honeymoon period of a relationship has worn off, if one of you is on the spectrum and the other is neurologically typical, you will have found it hard to communicate or understand each other – because one of you is driven by being rational and the other by emotions. With the pressures of young children or unruly teenagers, the gap will have grown. You will have categorised each other as 'difficult' and maybe stopped trying to communicate. In this atmosphere, it is easy to conclude you are 'too different' or your marriage was a 'mistake' – so far so familiar. However, while neurologically typical people can manage an affair for months and sometimes years, many men and women on the spectrum are quickly overloaded. (Please don't take this as a hard and fast rule as every person on the spectrum is different and, similarly, no two neurologically typical people are the same either.)

When Tony, forty-eight, came to his wife Anna and told her that their marriage wasn't working and they should separate, she was shocked. 'I knew he wasn't happy but I put that down to trouble at work and stress in general. He does work extremely hard,' she explained. 'But what threw me was his coldness and how he refused to discuss the reasons why he wanted to leave. When I asked if there was anybody else he swore blind that there wasn't.'

'I just wanted to close down the conversation. The marriage was over. What was the point of talking about it? Everybody would just get upset,' replied Tony. 'But yes, there was somebody else. Everything moved fast, too fast. I couldn't cope.'

A lot of this mindset and behaviour will be familiar to everyone who has been unfaithful and their partners. However, this is affair behaviour on steroids. More logical, more determined to move on and more disconnected from the other person's feelings (to the point of not understanding, beyond in a headline manner, what they might be).

While Anna was upset about the affair, it was – in particular – the break-up that she found a barrier to reconciliation:

'I could understand why you could fall in love with someone else but to be quite so unfeeling about the impact on me... What kind of man are you?' she asked him.

However, as we talked about their marriage before the affair, she had to recognise that he had often been disconnected and that she had focused instead on their children.

'I have been closing my eyes to lots of behaviours I didn't like – because I took them for granted, but I can't go back to that marriage.'

If you are wondering if you might be on the spectrum, please read more about it. There are also lots of autism 'pride' websites where people offer advice and support of an unapologetic kind. And there's nothing wrong with being on the spectrum; you're just different. However, it helps to understand the difference and to consider communicating in different ways with neurologically typical people.

Be reassured that the brain is plastic – not fixed – and you can teach yourself to be more aware of your own feelings (and name them). The Feelings Diary from Chapter One is a good start. Understanding your own emotions is an important step to being aware of other people's and sharpening your empathy skills.

Mental-health issues

During my many years as a marital therapist, I have come across people who have been given a serious mental-health diagnosis in the aftermath of the discovery of an affair (or a series of them). However, it happens rarely. To give you some idea of how rarely: I would need both hands to count the times but probably not all my toes.

The most common diagnosis is bipolar disorder (sometimes called manic depression), which involves unusual swings in mood, energy and activity. It comes in several forms including bipolar I, bipolar II and cyclothymic disorder. I have also had clients given a diagnosis of borderline personality disorder: unstable emotions, a weak sense of self and a fear of abandonment. With borderline personality disorder, there is often a history of self-harm and three times more women than men are given this diagnosis (which leads some people to believe it is as much a cultural label as a medical issue). It is considered to affect 1.6 per cent of the population.

While I meet few people who have been given a mental-health diagnosis, I regularly get the partners of people who have had an affair asking me if their husband or wife has narcissistic personality disorder (NPD). Unfortunately, the 'tell-tale' signs bandied about on the internet are so broadly written that – in the mind of a distressed partner – they fit their errant spouse to a T. For example, lack of empathy, a sense of entitlement, excessive need for admiration, focus on appearance and taking advantage of people around them. It could be a description of possibly half of all people who've had an affair. Meanwhile, I have met only one client who has actually been diagnosed by a psychiatrist with NPD after having an affair.

If your relationship is in a dark place, it could be that your partner is begging you to speak to your doctor and 'find out what is going on'. I can understand why you might be resistant and know the stigmatisation attached to mental-health issues. However, your doctor will be able to refer you to a psychiatrist who will not make a diagnosis lightly. In most cases where the wife or husband thought of NPD, it was something else (normally a bipolar disorder). If you do get a diagnosis, there could be medication to help regulate your moods. If nothing is found, you will have taken your partner's fears seriously and that is important for beginning to rebuild trust.

EXERCISE: UNDERSTANDING YOUR SHADOW

This is an idea that comes from Jungian depth psychology. Carl Jung (1875–1961) was one of the founding fathers of psychoanalysis and he believed the parts of ourselves that we don't like or can't accept are repressed into our shadow side.

Imagine walking down the street and the sun is shining, you are not always aware of your shadow but it's part of you and there all the time. No matter how fast you try to run away, it will always keep up with you. You can go to bed and draw the curtains, but the next morning your shadow will follow you around again. It's the same with the unacknowledged and unacceptable parts of ourselves. We can keep busy, hide in our work or fill ourselves up with high-cholesterol foods and alcohol, but no matter what we do any unowned feelings are still there.

The shadow is featured a lot in literature. Perhaps the most famous example is Robert Louis Stevenson's story *Dr Jekyll and Mr Hyde.* Dr Jekyll is a well-respected healer while Mr Hyde represents his shadow and therefore his opposite: he tramples over a girl and kills a man. However, it is not just negatives that are repressed. Someone with low self-esteem might not be able to own their positive qualities. Staying with famous stories, in Charles Dickens's novel *A Christmas Carol*, Scrooge's shadow manifests in the shape of the ghost of Jacob Marley who warns about his miserly behaviour. In this case, Scrooge's conscience and empathy are in his shadow.

Another example of repressing talents would be down-playing your intelligence; also, I have many clients that cannot own their sexuality (so don't relax and completely enjoy lovemaking) or their personal agency to change (and become depressed).

The impact of repression

Just because we disown something doesn't mean it goes away. So what happens?

> ➤ You are plagued by free-floating anxiety because your unnamed fears are never that far from your consciousness.

➤ You become completely driven to achieve greater and greater goals but still don't feel a success – despite all the objective proof to the contrary. The repressed feelings of being a failure are still there.

➤ When you are tired and stressed, the disowned material explodes out – often with a force that takes you by surprise. This is particularly the case with anger or resentment.

➤ The technical term for the next option is 'projection'. The best way to explain is to use a classic news story that comes up time after time. The bishop or the priest who is forever preaching against the wickedness of homosexuality or fornication is found to be visiting gay clubs or hiring prostitutes. In effect, he has been trying to distance himself from his own unacceptable practices by policing other people. So how would this work in your case? Instead of accepting that you are, for example, angry, you monitor your partner for the slightest slip in this department, project your disgust and attack him or her. In the bible, this would be described as taking the speck out of your brother's eye rather than the plank out of your own.

➤ Conversely, if you are projecting good qualities onto other people, you can end up putting your partner on a pedestal and become a supplicant. Rather than owning your own strength and ability, you think he or she is virtuous, powerful and has all the answers.

➤ If there are large parts of your personality that you believe need to be hidden, life can become a performance. You end up living behind a mask or worrying 'if people saw the real me they would reject me'.

➤ Even though you can't put your finger on exactly what's wrong – because it is all in the unconscious – you don't feel whole. Something is missing. You're right. It's hiding in your shadow or being projected onto someone else.

The alternative

Instead of ignoring the forbidden parts of yourself or policing the bits of yourself that you dislike in other people, you can begin to integrate the positive and negative aspects of your personality, put down the mask and become a more rounded person. So what does integration look like?

➤ You become aware of what is hidden in your shadow.

➤ You accept that the emotions or behaviours that were forbidden, either explicitly or implicitly, by your parents are part of being human. For example, it's OK to be proud, to speak up for yourself, to get upset (or whatever else was taboo growing up).

➤ The shadow is created and perpetuated by splitting off everything into either good or bad: the good face we show to the world and bad face we hide away in the shadows. Accept the world is not black and white. Rage can be healthy in certain circumstances. Kinky sexual practices are fine if everyone consents and enjoys themselves. Self-sacrifice can be detrimental if taken to extreme. Through integration, for example, rage can be transformed into assertiveness (I will cover this in more depth in the next chapter), vulnerability into compassion for others, and arrogance into a healthy self-esteem.

➤ Although there will still be situations and emotions that make you uncomfortable, knowing the source is old material from your child-hood cuts it down to a more manageable size. At this point, you can self-soothe (by going for a long walk, taking a bath or writing in your journal) or simply endure – rather than taking your pain out on other people or swallowing it and harming yourself.

➤ Finally, you start to develop the ability to laugh and to not take everything so seriously.

Discover what's in your shadow

It's surprisingly easy to discover what's in your shadow. Here are three techniques:

➤ Ask your partner, your friends or family what they find difficult to deal with in you. Instead of getting defensive or justifying yourself, take what they say as a gift: the gift of knowledge.

➤ Think about what really drives you wild about your partner. Could you be policing them rather than facing your own defects in this department?

➤ Make a list of all the things that are guaranteed to get your back up. I will give a personal example: 'You're just like your father.' I have put a lot of energy into not being like him. What therapists would call becoming the anti-father (which is still about my father rather than discovering my own path). Instead of denying that the apple does not fall far from the tree, I am working on accepting the similarities – like being testy and difficult – rather than ignoring them (and getting upset with my father). So what's on your list?

How to resolve the unconscious drivers

It is easy to be overwhelmed by how much the past impacts on today and the amount of work that needs to be done in the future. Please don't be. First, give yourself some praise for recognising the issues and resolving to be different. Second, focus back on the issues at hand: helping your partner and yourself recover from your affair.

Tell the story of why you were unfaithful

Human beings are meaning-making machines. We make sense of the world through stories. When you were unable to come up with an answer to 'Why did I cheat?', your partner came up with his or her own answers. When you refused to tell your partner what happened during your affair, he or she will have made up his or her own stories – of romantic meals and passionate clinches – and ended up persecuting him or herself with not only what you did do but these fake memories of what he or she imagined. Telling the story of why you were unfaithful will begin to tackle both these problems.

When your affair was discovered, and you still had Affair Brain, you could have said things – and even blamed him or her for your affair – that caused more pain than the original infidelity. Go back through what you said during this period, correct your lies and apologise for casting any blame. Finally, share the main points that spoke to you from the last chapter (conscious) and this chapter (unconscious drivers). Ask for his or her observations. Answer questions and listen respectfully when he or she adds her opinions. This process will probably be an ongoing exercise rather than a one-off conversation.

Unwind the training

We are given a lot of messages as children – some verbal, many more non-verbal – that we have taken deep within ourselves and woven into our identity. We watch how our parents navigate conflict and learn by example – sadly, not always the most constructive of approaches. Our attitudes to feelings will be forged by the messages and examples we took in when we were young. I call this our training and some of it might still serve us well but it is also part of what got you into this crisis.

So how do you unwind the training? First, write down all the messages from your childhood. Your mother's favourite sayings. What your father warned against. Were there any proverbs that were popular in your family? Next imagine, when it comes to conflict, that someone carved the family motto above the front door. What would it be? For example: 'Least said soonest mended' or 'Don't upset your mother' or 'Just get on with it'. Finally, think about the unspoken messages: these were never said – but were rigorously enforced by turning on the family member that broke them or by ignoring him or her. For example: 'We don't need to talk about how we feel about each other, we know and that's enough' and 'Feelings are embarrassing' or 'Nobody is allowed to get angry in this family'.

In most families, the rules are kept in place by three blanket injunctions: Don't question (or think too deeply), Don't feel (too strongly) and Don't talk (about what is really going on). So the best way to unwind the training is to be aware of the rules and to override the injunctions by telling yourself: 'Think deeply, feel and talk.'

If there is one message that has been particularly harmful, you might like to find a mantra to combat it. I had a client, Giselle, who had been given some very negative messages by her parents: 'You're trouble' (because she questioned their rules), 'You'll never amount to anything' and 'Don't make such a fuss'. Despite having a good job with a multinational company, Giselle had trouble getting the recognition she deserved with the firm. At first sight, her mantra should have been something like 'You can do it' or 'You're a success' but it had to be something she could truly believe – rather than aspire to believing. So I crafted something else for Giselle. She had a tendency to fade into the background and not take the credit she deserved.

'Some small piece of work that I did has become the template for the whole European division and has been written up as an example of excellence. However, when it came to the monthly assessment and bonus, I didn't get one. I know that there have been problems and nobody was getting one but I thought I deserved something,' she told me.

'Have you said anything?' I asked.

As I expected, she shook her head. The messages 'Don't make a fuss' and 'You're trouble' were too strong.

So I suggested that her mantra should be 'Show up'. By which I meant, don't fade away, speak up and consider yourself worthy enough to have an opinion.

'"Show up". I can buy that.'

She did show up and questioned her bonus. Her superiors discovered how central she had been to their new European project and she got transferred to a department that more suited her talents.

'Now I've got to see if I can walk the walk as well as talk the talk,' she told me modestly.

'What do you have to do?'

'Show up.'

So think about your negative messages and find something that you truly believe in order to unwind the training.

Become more spiritual

Spirituality is a state of mind, an attitude, a way of being in the world that allows us to be aware of something bigger than us. You might call this greater power 'fate' or 'the collective unconscious' or 'ultimate reality' or God. Spirituality is about being caring, considerate and life-affirming without being tied to a particular set of scriptures or a specific church. You can connect to this 'something bigger' through meditations, mindfulness (attention to what is happening around you, smelling the coffee, watching the buds open and really tasting your food), being creative and by continual enquiry.

So how does spirituality help in the recovery from infidelity? It makes our heart open and vulnerable to other people and requires us to surrender the sense that we always have to be in charge of everything. We can embrace the idea that there is not one fixed outcome or one path but many which could be rewarding and fulfilling. Being more spiritual will help you deal better with suffering and setbacks. Instead of thinking something *ought* to happen, you are more likely to try and understand and accept what *is* happening.

If this resonates with you, I have some suggestions of books to read in the appendix.

Therapy

You don't have to understand your past, cope with the pain today and find a different way of living tomorrow all on your own. It is OK to ask for help. Men, in particular, carry a toxic burden that they have to solve their own problems (and I meet some women who also think getting therapy is a sign of weakness). However, I've found it really useful to have an outside eye from someone who says, 'Hang on, you seem determined not to look over there, I wonder why.' It's good not to feel so alone and to have a companion who has walked these paths before. I have benefited from different perspectives and new ideas. I believe you could find therapy helpful, too.

SUMMARY

→ Understanding is not excusing. However, it does allow you to tell your partner the conscious and unconscious drivers for your affair and set the record straight once and for all.

→ You might have behaved in ways that are harmful to others because of the harmful or abusive acts that were inflicted on you when you were a child.

→ Self-knowledge is a better guard against future destructive behaviour than simply telling yourself not to do something again and hoping for the best.

WORKING
ON YOUR
MARRIAGE

CHAPTER SEVEN
////////////////////////

IMPROVING COMMUNICATION

So far you have faced the crisis of discovery (or confession) and dealt with the immediate aftermath. You have looked past your justifications for the affair and sought answers for why you were unfaithful. Now, you are going to take this knowledge and begin to work on repairing your marriage (or if you are uncertain what you want, to improve your communication in order to be great co-parents).

So why is communication so important that I have devoted a whole chapter to the subject? It is impossible for two people to live together without falling out from time to time. Of course, in the honeymoon period, love smoothed out the edges, but couples still need ways to resolve disputes. In an ideal world, they would talk about the problems and find a solution that worked for both of them. Unfortunately, there are lots of other ways that might on the surface work but which store up problems for the future. For example, one partner swallowing his or her needs to keep everything sweet; or one partner guilting the other into going along with his or her plan; or perhaps one partner just steam-rollers over any objections.

So how good are the two of you at dealing with the problems that life throws up? What happens when one of you has a legitimate complaint? For example, your partner has put so much energy into raising the children and running the family that you feel the last priority (after the dog, the cat and the hamster), or sex has dwindled from plentiful to scarce. Back to my ideal world, you would speak up, you would feel heard and a better balance would be found. But as you know, we don't live in an ideal world. That's why I sum up why affairs happen with this equation:

Problem + Poor Communication + Temptation = Affair

You should have a good idea about the 'problem' part of the equation and in this chapter I focus on the 'poor communication' element. In some ways, this is the most important part of the book and although I have touched on this topic before it deserves a chapter of its own. You will need good communication skills to listen to each other's pain and upset, to resolve the problems stored up in your marriage (which led to the affair) and to try to build a new relationship (because the old one clearly no longer works).

Why was the communication poor?

I have spent almost thirty-five years counselling couples and I must have heard millions of arguments. In many ways, the sticking point is not the topic but the way people fight. Time and again, I have observed six common traps into which couples fall. In each case, I have one simple solution to turn it round.

Not really listening

In the worst-case scenario, one partner will interrupt the other. However, what I see far more often is waiting (somewhat patiently) for the other person to finish but not really listening. In the meantime, you are rehearsing your answers or getting ready to demolish your partner's point (before you have truly heard what it is).

Another common scenario is going 'yes, but' and putting mental brackets round the things your partner is saying. For example, one person says, 'You hardly ever leave work when you say you will' and the other thinks, 'But I mean to leave, so my good intentions count for something' and 'Often I have to stay because there is a crisis and only I can sort it and my job pays the bills, so you don't really have the right to give me so much grief'. With these handy brackets, you can hear the words but discount the feeling. So have you really listened?

Turn it around: Summarise what your partner has just said. Use as many of his or her words as possible – rather than softening the message (for example, substituting 'annoyed' for 'angry') or editorialising (for example, 'you *wrongly* believe'). In this way, you will make certain that you have truly understood and that you have not missed something important to your partner. When I use this technique with clients some people complain it slows down the discussion (or row), but as you will see later that's not a bad thing. You will recognise this as reflective listening, which I introduced in Chapter Three.

Making assumptions

Particularly after an affair – during which communication is probably at an all-time low – it is likely that both you and your partner will have drawn conclusions about each other's behaviour that are at best only partially true and possibly a complete fabrication. For example, your partner might say: 'You can't give up that woman/man.' How does he or she know? Is he or she a mind reader? Alternatively, you might tell your partner: 'The problem is that you are obsessed with her/him.' You might have drawn this conclusion from what happened in the past but is that a reliable predictor for the future? What would happen if you were able to put all the assumptions to one side? After all, our assumptions colour what we hear and make good communication more difficult.

Turn it around: One of my most common interventions in couple sessions – and one of my most powerful – is to ask: 'Can you turn that statement into a question?' Good questions start with who, why, what, where, how. So your statement to your partner – 'The problem is that you are obsessed with him/her' – could become the question: 'How do you feel about him/her?' or 'What would help you to stop thinking about him/her?' Alternatively, you could simply ask: 'Are you obsessed?' Your partner could reply: 'I am not obsessed, I am frightened.' It's a completely different feeling and a revelation which could change how the two of you approach the topic. If your partner asked you: 'What would it take for you to give up talking to the other woman/man?' you might reply: 'I have cut back dramatically and I know I should stop altogether as it is not good for any of us.' In this case, a question has elicited new information for your partner and explaining your position could have helped you understand it better. Whereas an assumption (wound up with an accusation) would have just made you defensive and closed down the conversation.

Cross-complaining

If I had a pound for every time I heard a couple fall into this trap, I would be a rich man. Your partner says: 'You didn't support me when your mother was disrespectful.' You respond: 'You have been so wound up with work that you have neglected the children.' In your mind, both of these issues might be connected but all you have achieved is throwing more fuel onto the fire. It is possible that you might be able to solve one of these issues, but two at the same time: impossible.

Turn it around: Don't go for a win. Even if you did somehow 'prove' that your partner is in the wrong or bludgeon him or her into withdrawing the criticism of your mother, you have achieved nothing more than a few seconds of satisfaction. Meanwhile, your partner is feeling alienated and angry. Cross-complaining might work for office politics – although I doubt it – but it won't work at home (if you want your partner to keep on loving you). At the bottom of this tactic is a fear of being 'wrong' and therefore 'bad' and even worse 'unlovable'. These are the fears of a small child who might find it hard to believe that it is possible to both admire you for being loyal to your mother and exasperated at the same time.

Skipping to action

Nobody likes arguing. So the temptation is to wrap things up as quickly as possible. Therefore, you come up with a handy solution, everything is sorted and you can breathe safely again. Staying with the mother-in-law example, perhaps she had commented on the aftermath of the affair – so you promise: 'I will ask her not to say anything again.' Unfortunately, by closing down the conversation, your partner does not feel truly heard. He or she doesn't believe that you care about his or her feelings. Worse still, you might not have properly understood what had triggered him or her – so you might have come up with the wrong solution. Ultimately, it would have been more powerful if the two of you had talked and listened. Perhaps your partner did not need a 'solution', just to have his or her upset acknowledged. Alternatively, you could find a way forward together. After all, two heads are better than one.

Turn it around: You can slow down the whole process by exploring and understanding before you move on to action. The best way is to ask questions: 'What did you find particularly upsetting?' or 'What would you like me to have done?' or 'How do we tackle it differently next time?' The questions will deepen the understanding and potentially prompt more questions. For example: 'How does this fall into the general pattern between me and my mother?'

Checking out

For some people, arguments are not only unpleasant but also de-skilling. Perhaps they get flooded with emotions and become overwhelmed. Whatever the reason, it feels safer to walk away or stay but close down (and either not respond or agree to anything for a quiet life). In the short term, the strategy can work. You have time to calm down. Your breathing returns to normal. Life can go on again. However, in the medium term, your partner is upset or distant (but in your book, silence or a false truce is better than an argument). The real problem is in the long term; nothing gets resolved. Your marriage gets steadily worse, until one of you has an affair or says: 'I love you but I'm not in love with you.'

Turn it around: Stay in the crucible of conflict for just a little bit longer. One of my most effective strategies for helping couples resolve arguments is to encourage them to argue for five or ten minutes longer than normal. If you are feeling overwhelmed, focus on your breathing and name the feelings to yourself. If you can tell yourself it is anxiety rather than panic, you could stay in the row for a bit longer. In this way, you will have done enough exploring and understanding to reach action and come up with a solution that is a win for both of you.

Not being assertive

When it comes to disagreements, there are three ways of resolving disputes. I covered two that don't work in the last chapter. Let me recap.

You could believe: my needs, wants and beliefs are of lesser importance and yours are of greater importance. It is not that you are a complete martyr but you hope that by pleasing other people they will return the favour. I call this being passive.

You could believe: my needs, wants and beliefs are of greater importance and yours are of lesser importance. It is not that you are a control freak but you are 'right' (all sensible people would agree with you), or your partner doesn't express an opinion and someone has to do it, so it might as well be you. I call this being domineering.

In most marriages, couples find a balance by being domineering in one area but passive in another. For example, he is in charge of money (and what he says goes) and she in charge of the children (and has the ultimate casting vote). It is possible to run along for years like this but resentment can build up or some change in circumstance can throw everything off balance.

Fortunately, there is a third way. It is what I am suggesting for your marriage going forward. I call it being assertive: my needs, wants and beliefs are important and so are yours. In fact, they are both *equally* important.

Turn it around: So how do you settle disputes? It is easy when one is domineering and the other is passive: the domineering partner gets his or her way! In order to be assertive, you will need to follow all my guidelines for good communication. You will need to listen, ask questions and stay in the crucible of conflict for longer.

I sum up being assertive with this mantra: *I can ask, you can say no and we can negotiate.* It sounds easy but it could be a revolution in your life. Especially if you were not brought up to ask for what you needed ('I want doesn't get' was a saying in my family) or nobody was interested in your requests so there was little point in asking. Equally, it is hard to say no if you're anxious your partner will stop loving you if you don't agree with him or her. Finally, if your parents argued like cat and dog or never disagreed in front of the children, you will not know how to negotiate.

So what is a good outcome for a negotiation? You could find a compromise (acceptable to both of you). You could have a trade (where you get something you want and your partner gets something he or she wants). Sometimes, it might take a while to find a solution, but that doesn't matter. You can agree to put the decision on hold for a while and come back to it again.

EXERCISE: WHAT WAS THE LEGITIMATE PROBLEM?

In order to try out the skills outlined above, I would like you to find one of the legitimate issues that might have contributed to you embarking on your affair (which you identified in the previous chapter). I don't want it to be too global. In fact, I want it to be something specific that is likely to come up time and time again. To give you a better idea of what I mean, I have a case study.

Returning to Christopher, who we met in Chapter Six, one of his global problems was he did not feel 'supported' by his wife, Connie. When he'd told her in the counselling sessions, Connie got upset because she believed that she did 'support him' (despite his 'crazy' hours at work). So we looked at something specific and repeatable: Friday nights.

Connie liked to have a family meal and time for the two of them to be together (if only one evening a week). Christopher would have good intentions of leaving at a reasonable time on Friday but could get high-jacked by colleagues with pressing problems. When she got upset and criticised him for not being on time, he would feel misunderstood, his good intentions denied and therefore 'unsupported' in his work.

Once he had found a clear example of the problem and explained how it fed into the bigger picture, we could focus on improving the Friday-night experience for both of them. They could use the skills they had been learning: listening, being allowed to say no, asking questions and negotiating to resolve this particular dispute (and make a giant leap forward with the underlying issue).

So what could be one of your legitimate issues with your marriage to discuss with your partner? How could you make it specific rather than something global (where you could easily get bogged down in definitions)?

What would happen if you used the ideas in this chapter to tackle this issue?

//

A new way of looking at communication

According to an idea called transactional analysis (TA) – developed by Canadian-born psychiatrist Eric Berne in the nineteen-fifties – we have three parts to our personality: Parent, Adult and Child. None of these ways of communicating, or modes of being, is better than the other. We need them all.

Child is the source of our intuition, creativity and play (which helps us unwind, connect and facilitate sex). We also sometimes need to parent our partner, from time to time, and look after him or her when ill or going through a tough patch. The problem is when we get stuck in one particular mode, for example, repeatedly parent (by which I mean organising or trying to control) our partner, because he or she will repeatedly respond like a child.

To understand the full power of TA, I need to explain that Parent is divided into two parts: Nurturing and Critical. Child is also divided into two parts: these are called Free (which is the positive part I've already described) and Adapted (which includes rebelling, playing the martyr, whining, manipulating, sulking, switching off, acting defensive, passive-aggressive behaviour, etc.). Although there is a small place in any relationship for a bit of Critical Parent (because some behaviour is unacceptable) and for a bit of Adapted Child (because some of these behaviours can sometimes be understandable), in the aftermath of an affair, couples can easily get trapped in this dynamic. See the diagram on the facing page.

Becoming the critical parent

If you behave like a Critical Parent, your partner will automatically respond as an Adapted Child. Worse still, his or her Adapted Child can easily tip over into Critical Parent mode and that will send you into Adapted Child yourself (and, for example, you will become defensive). Although each partner will have a role that they are most comfortable playing, I like to think of it as a tennis match with you taking it in turns to serve and return. Critical Parent and Adapted Child is a game that can be played for hours, days or months and come to dominate your relationship.

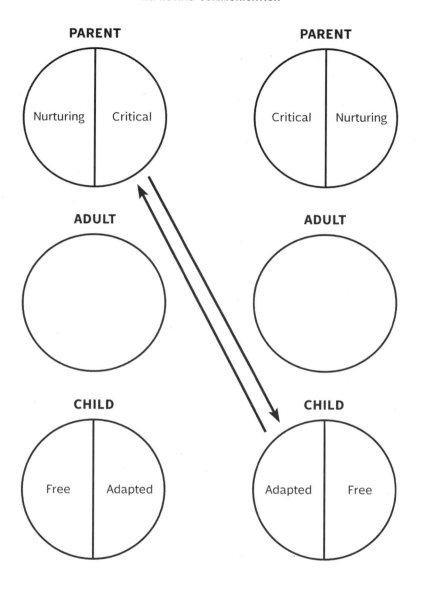

PARENT **PARENT**

Nurturing | Critical Critical | Nurturing

ADULT **ADULT**

CHILD **CHILD**

Free | Adapted Adapted | Free

Robert, forty-two, felt criticised by his wife all the time. 'Everything has to be planned and researched to get the best possible experience for our daughter – to avoid the latest disease and to buy the right organic sock. It's like some multi-layered complex project. If I try and help to get our daughter ready, my wife will say, "You'll only get it wrong, so leave it to me." I don't think I'm useless but I am by the current standards, which are high and unknowable.' So while his wife is being a Critical Parent, he is acting like an Adapted Child – by being passive-aggressive – and starting an affair. 'My wife and I only have sex every eighteen months – which feels like the tolling of the executioner's bell and I need human contact.'

Turn it round: Although it is very tempting to criticise your partner and point out his or her failings, it will just prompt sulking, self-justification or more rebellion. The answer is to move into Adult because this will promote some adult behaviour from your partner. The Adult mode is problem-solving and asks questions which start with: who, what, why, when, how. For example, Robert could have asked: 'How can we solve the problem of our sex life being infrequent?' Alternatively, he could have asked: 'What could I do to help you feel more in the mood for sex?' He could have given his view of childhood (kids are resilient and can be fitted into other activities), rather than something that needs to be constantly centre stage or a problem to be micromanaged (her vision). Both views are equally valid but cannot be discussed unless Robert is prepared to share his opinions and stand his ground (which is Adult) rather than detaching and people-pleasing to avoid his wife's irritation (which is Adapted Child).

Becoming the nurturing parent

Your partner is having a hard time recovering from your affair. He or she is depressed, finds life meaningless or his or her self-esteem is rock-bottom. So isn't it natural to be sympathetic and try to help (especially as you triggered the crisis)?

Although this trap is 100 per cent better than Critical Parent, there is a huge problem with being Nurturing Parent. You are still trying to manage your partner and, in the nicest way possible, run his or her life. The tell-tale signs that you're using the Nurturing Parent mode is that you feel like you're treading on eggshells and your partner keeps accusing you of being patronising.

Maggie, in her early forties, was determined to change and win a second chance for her marriage – even though her husband could not give up the other woman. When her husband wanted time away from both Maggie and his mistress, she researched and found him temporary bed and breakfasts. When he asked her what she wanted for her birthday, she asked him to meditate every day (because she'd found it helpful herself). She phoned up his parents to organise weekends away for her husband with them going too. Of course, it was better than shouting at him. However, Nurturing Parent is still part of Parent and it's easy to slip across to Critical Parent – especially when Maggie's husband didn't appreciate her efforts.

Turn it around: It's difficult enough to run our own lives and know what is best for ourselves, and almost impossible to do for somebody else. In counselling, Maggie started to examine her behaviour and discovered it wasn't quite so altruistic. 'Yes I wanted him to have peace from the meditation and space alone and time with his mother – who is showing the early signs of dementia – but I hoped they would all help him come back to me. His mother will remind him of the importance of family. He will miss me and the children when he's alone – rather than with *her*. With a more peaceful mind, could he think straight and make the right choice?' However, by being controlling, in the nicest possible way, she was encouraging her husband to go into Adapted Child and sulk, throw tantrums and rebel.

Instead Maggie needed to move into Adult and, by doing so, encourage her husband to switch to Adult, too. In this way, she could listen to his issues and he could hear her distress (rather than getting defensive). At this point, they could make a plan together for how to move forward – rather than Maggie trying to impose one.

EXERCISE: TRANSACTIONAL ANALYSIS IN ACTION

As I have explained, everybody has three parts to their personality: Parent, Adult and Child. While there are two types of parent communication (Critical and Nurturing) and two types of Child (Adapted – which is placating, protesting or appealing – and Free – which is spontaneous, creative and joyful), there is only one kind of Adult. We need all five modes as there are times when it is most appropriate to nurture or criticise (Parent mode); to be in problem solving mode (Adult mode); and to rebel, appease or just enjoy the moment (Child mode). The problem comes when we get stuck or spend too much time communicating in one particular way. So how do you use Transactional Analysis to improve your communication?

➤ *Week One:* Start by observing other people: when do they become Critical Parent ('I wouldn't if I was you…' or 'Why do you always…?') or Nurturing Parent ('Let me help you' or 'Don't worry') and when do they become Adapted Child ('It's not my fault' or 'I'm so, so sorry')? Look for the body language too: finger pointing (Critical Parent), nodding (Nurturing Parent), and downcast eyes, slumped shoulders and pouting (Adapted Child). How does one person's mode trigger the other's response?

➤ *Week Two:* Look for a moment when you've been in each of the five modes: Critical Parent, Nurturing Parent, Adult, Adapted Child and Free Child. The hardest to spot is Free Child, this is normally when you're laughing or excited (like playing sport or having sex).

➤ *Week Three:* Experiment with being in Adult mode, which asks questions like 'How?', 'When?', 'Why?' and 'What are the facts?' and has a clear and enquiring tone and open body language which involves good eye contact and active listening. How do other people react? Do they switch into adult mode too?

➤ *Week Four:* Focus on your relationship with your husband or wife and monitor the Critical Parent and Adapted Child transaction – as this is by far the most common. If your partner is critical, do not people-please or get rebellious but switch into Adult. You will be surprised at how quickly he or she will match you in Adult and how much this will improve your overall relationship. How do you stay in Adult? It is in the here and now (rather than going back over past examples or being too focused on the future). It is assertive and uses the mantra: 'I can ask, you can say no and we can negotiate.'

CASE STUDY

'The last four years of my thirteen-year marriage have been strained. My husband, a pharmacist, was robbed twice in six weeks at work. The latter with a gun to his head and demands to unlock the safe. After those incidents, his life changed dramatically. His personality changed from a loving man to a man who criticised me constantly. He would demean me in front of people. He would blame our parenting styles for causing problems in our marriage. He would also say that we were too different. He rejected all types of affection and we would go sometimes months (once a year and a half) with no sex. I would cry myself to sleep feeling so unloved. We began to fight. Loud, angry and nasty. I was so insecure. I became overweight, which heightened my insecurity.

'Finally he left the marriage for a week saying he didn't love me and didn't find me attractive any longer. He came back saying he would try. He did. Then it stopped. Sex was still not good. He either couldn't per-form, which I blamed on myself for being overweight. Or he would be callous and unloving while having sex. He would even hide my face with a pillow sometimes. I was miserable.

'Fast-forward the next few years. We stopped arguing. We lived together for the kids. I started to stand up for myself, but I felt unloved. There was no intimacy. He was still very critical. I would, every few months, explode and cry and say that I did not want to be in a loveless marriage and that he should leave if he didn't love me. He would go and then come back. He said that he did not need sex. He said that it was too expensive to divorce and that I really didn't bother him. Then he began going to the gym after work. He began mentioning a girl from work. I confronted him and he said that I was crazy and demanded too much from him. He hid his life from me, i.e. his phone, job. He even planned a trip to Vegas without me knowing. I was miserable.

'Then I fell into the trap of infidelity. I confided to a male friend about my misery. He also said that he was not happy. He began to flatter me and I ate it up. He listened to me. It became sexual. He said he was in love with me. It was funny. I was addicted to the high and companionship of the affair, but I never really fell in love. I always was waiting for my husband to come back to me. My affair partner was separating from his spouse. I felt that I needed to keep him interested just in case my husband left me.

'Next, I discovered a hidden envelope addressed to me with a date of twelve months prior telling me of my husband's affair, unsigned. I confronted him and he told me that he'd been having an affair for the last year with someone from work, fifteen years younger. I was relieved to discover this because it caused us to finally talk. He did not disclose much that day nor did I want him to. I also did not disclose my affair thinking he would just take that as a way out of the marriage. He said upon discovery that he wanted out of the marriage anyway because he knew I would never forgive/trust him again. We decided to live together until the shock wore off for the sake of the kids. But then, I discovered emails and photos and how entrenched he was. I also discovered another woman from years earlier.

'I was shocked and in pain. I wanted him to break it off but he said he did not want to lose her friendship in case the marriage didn't work out. Meanwhile, my AP (affair partner) and I stopped the sexual and emotional aspect of our relationship and he became the support I needed through this. I was crying to him over the pain I was in and how much I loved my husband.

'I finally demanded he end the relationship with the AP or leave. And I needed full disclosure. He did. We both disclosed our affairs. We both decided to give our marriage another try.

'It is hard. But he is going to counselling and it has made him see how awful he was to me. Our relationship has been through hell but it is now in recovery. Would I go through these last few years again? Our present-day marriage is filled with a renewed respect, honesty and love, so yes I believe I would.

'He was hurting and turned away from me. I took it personally and turned away from him. We got into a nasty cycle of nastiness. We both turned away from our marriage even though we loved each other completely. It has only been four months since discovery. I have triggers and bad days. I don't completely trust him. But we talk constantly about our feelings. He is completely transparent. I am too. We are intimate almost every day. I have read numerous books (many of yours) and I am also going to counselling.

'Ironically, I feel that we are blessed and God has given us both another chance. In fact, I feel sad for some of my friends' marriages who I feel are just as stagnant as my own.'

My reply

Thank you for sharing your experiences and giving others some inspiration. It shows what is possible when you are honest (with yourselves and each other), talk everything through and develop good communication skills.

///////////////////////////////////////

The Drama Triangle

This idea was developed by the Transactional Analysis therapist Stephen Karpman, who outlined three roles that people play in difficult situations. They are Victim, Rescuer and Persecutor (see diagram). As you will discover, the Drama Triangle is particularly useful in the recovery from infidelity.

You will recognise this triangle from the beginning of your affair. You were in the Victim role: you could do nothing right, you got no

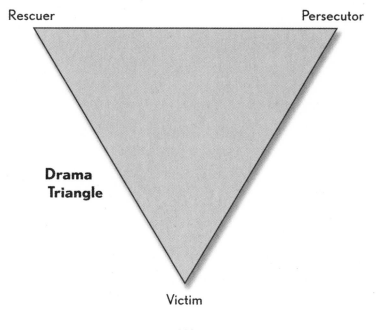

Rescuer   Persecutor

**Drama
Triangle**

Victim

thanks for anything and you were powerless to make any changes. Meanwhile, your partner was in the Persecutor position. He or she was critical, punishing or withholding. Along came your affair partner into the Rescuer role and helped you cope with the pain, provided moments of pure pleasure and the promise of better times in the future. However, none of the positions are stable and it is easy for all three of you to move round the triangle. Your affair partner will see him or herself as the Victim – after all, 'You say you love me but you are doing nothing to make our love a reality.' In other words, he or she wants you to be the Rescuer but finds you in the Persecutor position because you 'don't know what you want' or 'don't have the guts to follow through' or 'don't really care'. Once the affair is discovered, your partner becomes the Victim and your affair partner is the Persecutor and you have been cast as the Rescuer (who is supposed to say, 'It meant nothing' and 'I want you' and 'I will do anything to win you back').

Even when your affair partner is out of the picture, you and your partner will still hurtle round the three positions on the drama triangle. Let me explain how. He or she will be upset, you will try and rescue him or her; when all your efforts to make everything better fail, you will lose your patience, snap and get angry. Guess what? You are in the Persecutor role again. Alternatively, your partner is triggered and ranting about the injustice of the world, your wickedness and the impossibility of ever getting over it. He or she has now become the Persecutor and you are the Victim ('Nobody understands how hard I am trying', 'Everybody hates me, so I might as well go into the garden and eat worms'). Eventually, one or the other of you will play the Rescuer and a temporary truce will be found – until the next time. As you have discovered, it is possible to get stuck in the Drama Triangle. Fortunately, there is an alternative.

Moving on to the Winner's Triangle

This next idea is credited to another TA trainer, called Acey Choy (however, she claims not to have invented it but rather to have found it, although she can't remember where). I like the concept because it provides not only clues about how to break the Drama Triangle but also a clear goal for the future. So what does the Winner's Triangle involve? In Choy's version, the positions are Assertive (instead of Persecutor) and Caring (instead of Rescuing) and Vulnerable (instead of Victim). However, when I have used the triangle in the aftermath of an affair, the discoverer of the affair could not relate to Vulnerable as a place in the Winner's Triangle (see diagram below). After their partner had an affair, they felt incredibly vulnerable. They realised that one decision to 'cheat' could mean losing their home, a big chunk of monthly income and their children losing a full-time parent. Of course, they knew all about Vulnerable. How could there be anything good about 'vulnerable'?

Despite all the negative connotations of Vulnerable (as weak and helpless), there is a positive side to the word — which is what Choy meant. Vulnerable means open. It is the opposite of victim, which is closed. You are either curled up in a ball (saying, 'Don't hurt me') or walking away (shouting over your shoulder, 'Nothing will ever hurt me again').

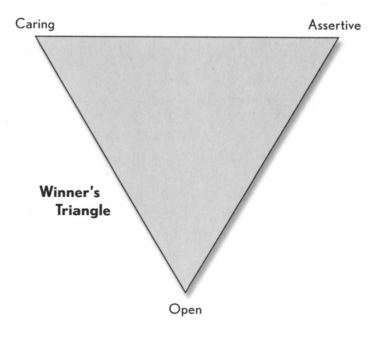

So to avoid any confusion, I have 'Open' as the goal of the Winner's Triangle.

When I did the Winner's Triangle with Angela and David, a couple in their early fifties recovering from his affair, he immediately asked: 'But isn't a Rescuer going to be caring? I don't understand the difference.' David had an affair with a work colleague and despite two previous attempts at counselling (with other therapists) they were still trying to recover almost five years after he finally admitted to being unfaithful. They had found the Drama Triangle very useful because when Angela was upset, David would try and take the pain away and make everything all right. In effect, Angela would start as the Victim and David as the Rescuer.

'If only I could find a way to answer her questions about when and why the affair happened. But it was so long ago, I can't remember when it tipped over from colleagues talking about "what I did over the weekend" to discussing inappropriate things like "my unhappiness with Angela" or what exactly I did say,' he explained.

At this point, he would get frustrated with himself (for not being able to rescue) and with her (for asking for the impossible) and consumed with guilt (because he caused the pain and therefore felt responsible for healing it). He would act out his feelings by becoming angry and defensive. Returning to the Drama Triangle, he would become the Persecutor – which would make Angela angry too: 'How dare he treat me like this? I'd get upset about all the years I'd lost out of my marriage and I'd feel stupid for putting up with some of his bad behaviour before all this started. Eventually, I would lose my temper and say spiteful and horrible things.' At this point, David would switch off and withdraw – pursued by Angela. She had become the Persecutor and, in his mind, David felt the Victim.

'A Rescuer is like a knight in armour who sweeps the victim off her feet and "saves" her,' I explained. 'But you can't "save" her or "make it all right" because some of the problems are about her stuff.'

'Because lots of this is about how I feel about myself because the other woman was younger and prettier,' Angela chipped in.

'In the Winner's Triangle, you just need to care – which doesn't involve getting frustrated and switching off,' I explained to David.

Next, I turned to Angela: 'In many ways, your last statement begins to show the difference between Victim and Open. First of all, a victim blames other people – for example, "You destroyed my confidence" or "You made me hate my body". Obviously, this is a tough place to be. I picture it as down on the floor. Sadly, to compensate, people swing to wonderful: "I'm a special creation" and "Nothing can touch me". I picture this as up in the air.'

Angela nodded, she could recognise those two extremes.

'What I'm looking for is the opposite of "nothing is going to hurt me again", which might be the polar opposite of Victim but can be equally unhelpful. Essentially, there is a middle place between Victim and untouchable. I would like you to be Open. Open to looking at your part of the problem and taking your part of the responsibility rather than simply blaming.'

I also find some people in the Victim corner are tempted to run away and start a new relationship, which at the time seems a solution but, more often than not, means finding a new Rescuer and perpetuating the Drama Triangle.

Although in the Winner's Triangle, Open replaces Victim, Caring replaces Rescuer, and Assertive replaces Persecutor, everybody needs each of these three attributes. Therefore, while switching positions on the Drama Triangle is destructive, switching positions on the Winner's Triangle is constructive.

The Skills Triangle

Now I've identified the problem (the Drama Triangle) and the goal (the Winner's Triangle), the next question is: how do we get there? I came up with this triangle, and as the name suggests: you need skills. So let's have a look at them:

Hopefully, you'll have let out a sigh of relief because you've already begun to acquire these skills. I have already covered negotiating and listening. I introduced the concept of adult-to-adult conversations – who, why, what, how questions – which is central to problem-solving. In effect, adult to adult is an equal relationship rather than parent and child – which is fundamentally unequal – and can easily become rescuer and victim.

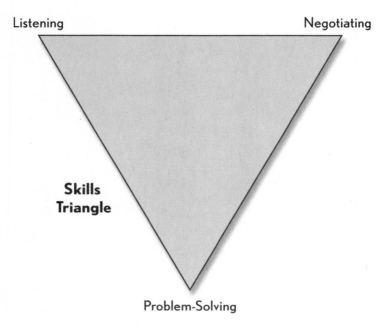

Listening

Negotiating

**Skills
Triangle**

Problem-Solving

So returning to David and Angela, David only had to *listen* to Angela to demonstrate that he did care about her feelings and was truly sorry for his infidelity. For Angela, instead of waiting for David to make her feel better, she could be empowered and start to look at how to solve the problem herself. Finally, they could be two equal partners in resolving their marriage problems.

Let's recap the three triangles and the journey of each particular corner:

Drama	⟶	Winner	⟶	Skills
Victim	⟶	Open	⟶	Problem-Solving
Rescuer	⟶	Caring	⟶	Listening
Persecutor	⟶	Assertive	⟶	Negotiating

If you're trapped in the Drama Triangle, you will have played every role but there will be one position to which you will naturally gravitate. Therefore, focus on that journey, the goal in the Winner's Triangle, and think about how you could improve the relevant skill in the final triangle. If you are like most people who have had an affair, you will feel so guilty for the pain caused to your husband or wife that you will want to rescue. So focus on being caring and the skill of listening.

In my opinion, the three most loving words in the English language are not 'I love you' (although they are great) but 'tell me more'. It is really loving to ask your partner to 'tell me more' when you know it's going to be painful and distressing. It shows that your partner is acceptable not only when he or she is being nice (on best behaviour), but even when upset, crying and what he or she fears is unattractive. So show you can listen and the next time your partner complains or is angry, listen and then ask: 'Is there more?' (in a loving and open manner).

EXERCISE: TEN QUESTIONS TO DESIGN YOUR NEW MARRIAGE

If your discussions about a possible future together get bogged down by the pain of your affair, you will find this structure particularly helpful. The technique is called Appreciative Inquiry – and I introduced it in Chapter One. It is used by businesses undergoing a transformation. Traditionally, they would ask: 'What doesn't work?' (which made their employees defensive and blame each other), but changing the question to: 'What works and how do we build on it?' created a positive atmosphere (where staff were open and creative).

With a greater knowledge of the causes of your affair and better communication skills, it's time to return to Appreciative Inquiry and discuss how you would like your new relationship to look.

It has four parts – discover, dream, design and deliver – and there are specific questions for each one. While you're doing the exercise, if something about the affair comes up, write it down to discuss later. The aim is to stay with the positives.

Set it up

Hold hands and look into each other's eyes. Harvard psychologist Zick Rubin found couples in love spend 75 per cent of their time looking into each other's eyes – rather than the usual 30 to 60 per cent. I would like you to spend at least five minutes doing this. Keeping eye contact is both intimate and challenging, so if your partner gets emotional squeeze his or her hand. Use the time to think about the qualities that you admire in your partner.

When one of you is ready, start to share your thoughts. One or two word qualities work best – for example: courage, strength, compassion, kindness, beautiful eyes – there is no need to explain. Take your time. It is OK to pause and see what comes to mind but I would like at least five qualities. If you are on the receiving end, please accept the compliment – even though you might normally demur or run yourself down – by just saying thank you. At this point, swap over roles.

Once you have finished this warm-up, and are in a positive mood, you can start asking and answering my ten questions.

■ DISCOVER

1. When we first met, what made you think that I was someone special?

Why: It is good to remember what brought the two of you together and your original connection.

Take it further: Remember funny or touching incidents from your courtship. Think about what you did that helped to build the connection.

2. When are we at our best together?

Why: Love is built as much from overcoming obstacles as from sharing good times. What kinds of circumstances bring out the best in your relationship?

Take it further: How do your different strengths complement each other and help make your marriage stronger?

3. In your opinion, what was the most romantic day we have spent together?

Why: It is likely that each of you will come up with different days. Rather than assuming your partner's take on romance is the same as yours, here is a chance to find out what builds connection for him or her.

Take it further: Go over this day in as much detail as possible so you not only enjoy the trip down memory lane but also discover the exact events or actions that made it so special.

4. What do you enjoy most about our lovemaking?

Why: It is embarrassing to talk about sex and that's why I have put in this question, so you don't conspire together to overlook it.

Take it further: It's really important to keep this conversation positive – because sex can make us feel particularly vulnerable. If you find yourself thinking about what you DON'T like, flip it over. For example, if you don't like rushed sex answer: 'I like it when we take our time' (even if you can't remember the last time it was like this!).

▇ DREAM

5. What would be the perfect day for you, from waking up to falling asleep?

Why: This question is designed to help you think about some goals for changing your relationship.

Take it further: Don't censor yourself. It doesn't matter if any of the dreams are hard to achieve. It's important, at this stage, to listen to each other and be creative together. Anything is possible, you will think about practical matters later.

6. What ambitions have you still got to achieve?

Why: One of the biggest problems in midlife is feeling bored and trapped. Setting fresh goals can help your life become meaningful and focused again.

Take it further: Ask your partner: how can I help you with your ambitions? Instead of your beloved feeling alone or even held back, you can start to become a team. Remember you are only asking how to help your partner achieve the goal, not resolve it for him or her.

7. If we had all the time in the world, what would you like us to do more of together?

Why: This question allows you to look into the future. Contrary to popular belief, the older we become, the happier we are. The Office for National Statistics collected data from 300,000 people and found life satisfaction improving from sixty-plus and the age group with the most positive ratings were aged seventy to seventy-four.

Take it further: Encourage each other in a flight of fantasy by saying: 'Yes and another thing we could do...'

▣ DESIGN

8. How can we make these dreams come true?

Why: After discovering what works currently in your relationship and dreaming of how it might be in the future, comes the more practical part.

Take it further: Think about your skills that might help in the project. For example, one of you might be good at research and the other at planning.

9. What could the obstacles be and how can we overcome them?

Why: You know all the problems, like lack of time; the idea is to spend less time on those and more on how to carve off enough emotional space and energy for your relationship.

Take it further: If you find yourself slipping into old negative patterns or feeling anxious, hold hands and take a few deep breaths together. It is amazing how this will help you calm down and focus back on the pleasure of being together right here and right now.

▣ DELIVER

10. What are the next steps each of us is going to take?

Why: According to the ancient Chinese philosopher, Lao Tzu (b. 601 BC): 'A journey of a thousand miles begins with a single step.' You are going to commit to the journey ahead by thinking about what each of you can do to start it.

Take it further: Discuss what you have enjoyed about this experience and how you can build on it in the future. Perhaps Appreciative Inquiry could be used for other things in your life.

Afterwards

Endings are just as important as beginnings. So spend some time looking into each other's eyes again. You could finish off by taking it in turns to list all the things for which you are grateful. These will range from the profound to the silly. For example: good health, time together, chocolate and long walks. Say thank you and have a hug, long enough for both of you to relax and melt into each other.

SUMMARY

→ Successful relationships need skills and the most important one is good communication.

→ There are many similarities between being assertive, in the Adult-to-Adult mode and in the Winner's Triangle.

→ They all involve expressing your own needs, listening to your partner's and negotiating.

CHAPTER EIGHT

////////////////////

REBUILDING TRUST AND DESIRE

Congratulations on getting to the final chapter of this book. If you have been engaging with the ideas and doing the exercises, you will have been on a big journey. You have the beginnings of a vision for your new marriage and, more importantly, the skills to build it. However, I will not be at all surprised if you still have doubts about the future. There will be times when you will be overwhelmed by the enormity of what you have done and the magnitude of the task ahead. Sometimes it will feel that the promised land of recovery is still a long way off or the entrance is barred. At these moments, you will ache for one or all of the following: hope, forgiveness and trust.

Three building blocks for the future

I have spent thirty-five years helping couples recover from affairs and have run a website with many articles about infidelity for almost fifteen years. During this time, I have been asked a lot of questions but there are three themes that come up over and over again. They are:

➤ 'Is there any hope for us?'

➤ 'Will my partner ever forgive me?' or 'Can I forgive my partner?'

➤ 'If my partner can't trust me, what's the point of carrying on?' or 'If I can't trust my partner, how can I even begin to repair my marriage?'

So let's look at these questions and the three qualities for which you long.

Hope

Hope is rather a mixed blessing. It can make you close your eyes to inconvenient facts. For example: your affair partner has an angry and vindictive ex who would do everything in his or her power to ruin any future relationships. You can swing from unrealistic optimism ('something will turn up' or 'tomorrow is another day') through to a debilitating hopelessness (which denies the solid progress that has been made and makes you dwell on words like 'never' and 'always'). Meanwhile, hope is necessary in times of adversity – and recovering from an affair certainly fits that category.

Whether you accept or deny, hope will have a big impact on your mood. If you are stuck in a feeling hopeless phase, it could be that you are depressed and need to see your doctor. If you find that your moods swing back and forth (and that's a regular pattern that goes back to before the affair), I would also consult your doctor.

However, it's normal to have ups and downs in recovery. What would happen if you accepted your mood today and looked at what your feelings were trying to tell you and what you needed to learn?

My answer: When someone asks 'Is there hope?', I always say: 'Yes', but only if certain conditions are met. Are you learning about yourself? Are you learning about life in general? Are you changing? If the answer to these questions is yes, I am full of hope. If someone asks me: 'Do you believe people can change?' which is another variation on 'Is there hope?' I also answer: 'Yes'. If I didn't think people could change, I wouldn't be a therapist. There are plenty of other things I could do with my life! What people are often asking me is: 'Can my partner change?' That's a more complicated question but if you change, that will change the dynamic in your relationship and that can bring about change.

Forgiveness

Wouldn't it be wonderful if your partner could only forgive you, the two of you could put the affair behind you and life could return to normal? However, forgiveness requires strength and courage. My guess is that your affair has turned your partner's life upside down, made him or her question everything that he or she believed in and shown just how vulnerable he or she is. It is not a situation that promotes either strength or courage. Even worse, your partner might feel that forgiveness will put him or her at further risk. It can be seen as condoning your behaviour, giving permission for future transgressions or a free pass to continue an affair. I always counsel against trying to forgive too soon – especially when the wounds are still fresh. So how can you help your partner forgive you?

First off, you can give a heartfelt apology. It involves identifying the behaviour that you regret (this might be the whole affair or something specific like giving your affair partner a lift in your car), identifying the impact on your partner (for example, you violated family space and made your partner angry), and committing to changing and not repeating this behaviour. You can give extra credence to your claim by outlining what you are doing differently (for example, 'I am reading a book about affairs and learning why I had an affair'). Without you making a sincere apology – on a regular basis – your partner will feel he or she could lose face by forgiving.

Secondly, you can understand why your partner is having a problem forgiving. It's especially hard if your betrayal taps into memories of similar childhood experiences and reawakens a dormant reservoir of pain. For example, your wife's father was charming on the surface but put his own pleasures above the needs of his family. Perhaps your husband's mother was unreliable and would sink into depression and he thought he had finally found a woman who would put him first. If you identify the bigger patterns, you will be more patient with your partner and less likely to push for forgiveness (as some kind of magical once and for ever solution). Once the pressure is off, your partner will be able to find forgiveness in his or her own time.

Thirdly, you can forgive your partner for his or her transgressions. What do I mean by this? Once you have stripped away the justifications and rationalisations for the affair (and apologised for them), you will be left with some legitimate issues. For example, your partner always sided with his or her mother and let her belittle you. Instead of holding on to this resentment, you could understand why, for example, standing up to his or her mother was difficult, and forgive your partner. After all, we all have different approaches to the world and different temperaments.

If *you* forgive, you model the behaviour that you seek and encourage your partner to move towards forgiveness, too.

My answer: If it is the discoverer of the affair asking: 'How do I forgive?', I explain that forgiveness is a decision rather than a feeling. I see it less as a gift to their unfaithful partner but more as one to themselves. Holding on to grudges keeps us in the victim mode and keeps the offender at the centre of our life. By contrast, forgiveness can set us free (but only when it feels safe to do so).

If it is the person who had the affair asking, 'Will I ever be forgiven?' I ask him or her to focus on not only making amends but also working on him or herself. 'So have you looked at why being in debt to your partner is so painful?' 'Does it bring up the hurtful or harsh behaviour of one of your parents?' 'Has your affair and its discovery tapped into a reservoir of your childhood pain?' 'Are you asking your partner to forgive, so you don't have to face the old wounds?' Instead of focusing on how your partner could be different (which is not in your gift) think about what you could do differently (which is something you can control). 'So what could you do to help yourself cope in this difficult phase between discovery and recovery?'

Finally, what do I say to a couple after an affair? Forgiveness should not be confused with a pardon. You can forgive someone and at the same time require restitution.

Trust

Trust is something that we take for granted – a bit like electricity – we only notice it when it's gone (or there's a power cut). As you have probably discovered, trust is one of the cornerstones of a relationship. Your partner does not want to be continually checking up on you; and you don't want to be looking over your shoulder and thinking how your behaviour might be interpreted. No wonder you are desperate to be trusted again.

When you're in a dark place, trust can seem like the magic bullet to make everything right. Hopefully, however, you have learned that magic solutions normally make matters worse rather than better. Getting exasperated and demanding trust or getting angry and threatening to end the relationship if your partner can't trust, is a recipe for hopelessness and makes forgiveness harder. Ultimately, there's no alternative but to roll up your sleeves and do the hard work. So what might that involve?

It's important to understand that, unlike forgiveness, trust is not something that we can rationally choose. Whether we find it easy to trust or not is rooted deep in our character, our childhood and our life experience. If your partner was unable to trust that his or her parents would provide unconditional love or that the universe (or fate, God, whatever) would provide what he or she needs, trusting you will be tougher. However, if you understand the bigger picture – that it's not all about you – being cross-examined by your partner will not feel so personal and you can dial back your upset.

Fortunately, there are things that you can do to make yourself more trustworthy. Look at the following questions: do you tell the whole unvarnished truth? Are you being transparent about your diary and discussing potential problems in advance? Do you get defensive and angry or do other things that set back your partner? What could you do differently?

My answer: Discoverers are surprised at my answer to their complaint: 'I can't trust my partner.' I reply: 'Good.' Normally, it is too early and their partner has not earned the right to be trusted. Time and again, I see discoverers reach for trust – to try and make themselves feel better – but their partner still has an Affair Brain (see Chapter Four) or has not taken the truth drug (see Chapter One). There is some fresh discovery – sometimes something major and sometimes just an unreported unsolicited call from the affair partner – and the tender shoots of trust are destroyed. Each time this happens, it becomes harder to trust.

Instead, I ask discoverers to trust the *process*. By which I mean, the seven stages of recovery (Chapter Three). I have yet to meet a couple for whom stage two, 'Intense Questioning', and stage six, 'Despair – bodies float to the surface', do not shine a spotlight at the heart of their marriage. Along the way, by resolving both day-to-day issues and the causes of the infidelity, couples begin to trust they have the skills to not just survive but also to thrive.

When your partner believes you will speak up about problems – rather than bottling things up and being tempted – and that the two of you can overcome future obstacles together, it becomes much easier to trust.

In effect, trust comes at the end of recovery, not at the beginning.

EXERCISE: INGRAINED PROBLEMS

If you are following the ideas in this book, you should be over the initial crisis of discovery and generally doing better. However, there are two situations where your hard-won progress can easily be set back: when your partner is overwhelmed with anger or you are overwhelmed with shame. Sometimes, the two things can happen at the same time. Sounds familiar? If you have been trying to recover from infidelity for a long time, it is likely that both anger and shame have become ingrained in your relationship. Fortunately, I have some strategies to deal with this situation.

Your partner is angry

Anger is a natural human emotion and inevitable in the aftermath of an affair. From a therapist's point of view, anger is positive. The feelings are coming to the surface and can be dealt with, instead of being buried as resentment (which does much more harm to relationships). However, I understand it is horrible to be on the receiving end of a tirade of anger (perhaps with some abusive language thrown in for good measure). So what should you do? You will recognise the first part of the exercise because it is the same as dealing with anger in the immediate crisis after discovery. I have built on these foundations and added an extra layer to address the ingrained elements.

1. *Keep calm.* Take a few deep breaths. Focus on the air going into your nostrils and coming out of your mouth. Your partner's anger will not last for ever and there are things you can do to help it pass.

2. *Accept your partner's feeling.* Don't try and rescue your partner from his or her anger (or yourself). Remember the winner's and skills triangles in the previous chapter: you only have to care and you can do that by listening. If you try and challenge your partner's viewpoint – even if some of the things he or she is saying are wrong – he or she will think you are either being defensive or minimising his or her pain. You will just make him or her angrier. Remember, you just have to listen.

3. *Summarise your partner's main points.* In order to make your partner feel heard (and his or her feelings accepted), I would like you to summarise the main sources of the upset. Please remember to summarise rather than editorialise. An example of editorialising would be 'which you wrongly believe' or changing his or her words for nicer ones: instead of 'viscous' replacing it with 'unhelpful'. The second advantage of this approach is you will spend more time on what your partner is actually saying (rather than beginning to interpret, putting a worse spin on it and starting to panic) or preparing your defence.

4. *Ask about the feelings.* When your partner is calmer, ask about his or her feelings. It might be that what you perceive as anger is really sadness or resentment or a soul wound (your affair has torn at the roots of your partner's identity or beliefs about the world).

5. *Who is your partner angry with?* It could be that your partner is angry with him or herself or your affair partner or his or her mother or something he or she heard on the TV – as well as you. Because we are the centre of our worlds, we tend to think that all the anger or pain is caused by us. I have a mantra: *It's not all about me.* Yes, your partner is angry with you but also at a whole lot of other people (including him or herself). Remembering this mantra will make you a little less overwhelmed, a little less defensive and a better listener.

6. *Apologise.* You can never apologise enough. Make it specific and targeted at the causes of the anger rather than a general 'I'm sorry'.

7. *Think about the roots of the anger.* When you understand more about the type of anger and the causes, you can think about the roots. For example, if it is resentment for all the energy you put into arranging dates with your affair partner, you can fix up a special night out with your husband or wife and book a babysitter. Tackling the roots of the anger is better than trying to divert the anger or play it down.

You are overwhelmed by shame

Shame is also a natural human emotion. We all feel it all the time. However, we are so keen to avoid it that we keep busy, distract ourselves or keep it at bay by trying to be perfect. In the aftermath of the affair, you are going to be more aware of shame. Not just the shame associated with the impact of your affair on your family but also the routine day-to-day shame of not being 'good enough' or making 'stupid' mistakes, or the negative images we have of our body, our age and our abilities.

Summing up, I am not surprised if you feel overwhelmed with shame, but fortunately I have some techniques to help.

1. *Accept the feeling.* You will recognise this one as I've covered it before. If you accept your partner's feelings are valid, you can extend the same courtesy to yourself. At this point, you might find the feeling is guilt (you have done a bad act) rather than shame (you are a bad person and therefore unlovable). It could also be anger or sadness or any number of other emotions. If you try and push the feeling down or go on the attack, you won't know what it is.

2. *Challenge the thoughts.* No apologies for repeating this idea again as I can't say this too often. There are probably all sorts of ideas flying around in your head which might not be true or may be an exaggeration. For example, 'We are back to square one' (when it is just a temporary setback) or 'I have ruined my partner's life' (ruined is a strong word and gives you almost God-like power over his or her life – at the worst you have ruined a section of it).

3. *Report the feelings.* Tell your partner: 'I am feeling shame.' Although you feel it all the time, you partner will not be aware. Time and again, when I help the partner who had the affair name his or her shame in my counselling room, the other partner is relieved and sometimes even pleased. He or she has worried that their partner does not seem to feel any shame (for where he or she stands) or that his or her pain is not taken seriously. The other advantage is that your partner will be more aware of the impact of his or her anger, constant questioning or insults and choose a less combative approach.

4. *Step away.* If you are about to be overwhelmed and become defensive, shut down completely or go on the attack, try taking a short break instead. Ask your partner: 'Can we take a short pause for a cup of tea or coffee?' Promise to come back in ten minutes or so and start the conversation again. It is crucial than you follow through and return to the conversation (or your partner will not cooperate the next time you are overwhelmed).

5. *Think about your old wounds.* It could be that the shame you feel today is reactivating old shame from the past. Did your parents use 'shame' to control you? Did teachers at school say, 'You'll never amount to anything'? Or perhaps you were bullied by fellow pupils or made to feel 'inadequate' by a former boyfriend or girlfriend. It is better to tackle the roots of the old shame rather than avoid the current shame. You might like to consider getting help from a therapist with this task.

CASE STUDY

'My situation is similar to many you probably have heard. I have been having an affair for almost two years now (one year, eight months). My wife found out about it the first summer after about three months when she questioned me and I came clean. I broke it off then, but got back together with her just a week after. My affair partner ended her marriage last June – it was a bad and abusive marriage and I don't feel our relationship was responsible for that divorce.

'I have been married to my wife for twenty-five years and we have two daughters – one is nineteen years old and now in college and the other is fourteen and in high school. I have felt that my sexual needs have never been met during my marriage and that is why I reached outside my marriage in the first place.

'The first affair I had was over seventeen years ago before my youngest daughter was born. I ended that affair and reconciled my marriage. After this current affair started, I have wondered if my sexual needs with my wife were ever really met or have I just been trying hard to get by for the sake of my daughters. My wife is a very loving mother and I do love her, but like you say… I am not IN love with her.

'My affair partner sent my wife a package basically outing our affair relationship so that I would either choose her and move forward with a divorce or choose my wife and reconcile my marriage. Again, the lies took over… and I told my wife I had broken up the affair but re-engaged with her (my affair partner) over last summer, and that it had ended just before she sent that package. The truth was that I had continued seeing her the entire time.

'My affair partner really wants to be with me, but wants me to take care of my situation (marriage) in a responsible way and take the time necessary to do it right. I have told her that I love her, but I'm very torn between leaving my wife and daughters to be with her and staying. I have beaten myself up for almost a year now and balancing time with my affair partner and the lies I have to tell have destroyed me, and had a detrimental effect on my relationship with my affair partner. Currently, my affair partner and I have decided to take a "step back" so I can deal with my struggles (she believes and hopes aimed at speaking to my wife and ending my marriage). Please help me… I still go back and forth in my head and can't decide what to do.

'One fear I have is that if I just end things with my affair partner and go back to my wife, my life and marriage will go back to the same old, same old and I will be right back where I started, wanting to look outside my marriage again. But if I divorce my wife my fear is my relationship with my daughters will be different, they will resent my drastic change to their lives, and I will regret breaking up my family.'

My reply

You're right I have heard this before. From the outside, however, it seems quite clear cut. Let's start with your affair partner – for me, putting together a package of evidence and sending it to your wife was manipulative and controlling (and, to be honest, cruel). I can understand why she might have lost patience with you but, in my book, this behaviour is unforgivable. If you 'reward' your affair partner by choosing her, you are encouraging more of it. Do you want to be married to this sort of woman? What is it going to be like when your daughters enter the picture? I doubt it will be pretty.

Furthermore, I think you are far too quick to gloss over the 'bad and abusive' marriage. Why was it bad? Why was it abusive? Let's start with the bad; I have yet to find a relationship where both parties don't bear lots of responsibility for the marriage reaching such dark places. As for abusive, your affair partner is not responsible for the abuse but why did she stay in it for so long? Often it is because she had been 'trained' to put up with such behaviour from a young age by abusive parents (either to each other or towards their children). If I am really putting my cards on the table, your behaviour towards her and all the lies and coming and going is heading towards the abusive. Yet she still wants more! So I suspect there is a lot of personal material that she needs to sort out. However, instead of doing the hard work, she is rushing to a happy ending in your arms. Without doing the work, I think she is likely to bring the horror show of her first marriage into her relationship with you (plus her unprocessed anger at you for mucking her around).

Let's move on to your marriage. You're right. You can't go back to the same old marriage and paper over the cracks. There is simply no sense in going round the same old merry-go-round again. The question is, could you have a different marriage with your wife? A new one with honesty about what you need. A new one where you do not bury your feelings. A new one where you are lovers as well as co-parents. What would your wife need before she would contemplate such a marriage? If she is up for a new marriage, what would it look like for her? Do your two visions have anything in common – beyond the children?

Before you can have any sort of conversation with your wife, you have to take the truth drug and tell her everything that has happened and clear up all the lies. When you do not tell the truth, you are not present and you can't be connected to anyone. Worse still, you end up lying to yourself, and if you're doing that how can you know what you want?

Next, you are putting the problems of your marriage down to sex... And you may well be right. However, I find there is often a lot more to unpack than just what happens in bed. Here's the problem: Men are trained not to listen to their heart (and sometimes they are told not to think too much – but just get on with it). But they are told to think a LOT about what their penis wants. (In fact, there is a whole industry called porn that reinforces the message that sex is of supreme importance to men.) So if you're not listening to your heart and your head, but you are tuned in to your penis, it's quite likely that a whole lot of problems that don't necessarily belong to your private parts end up registering there.

So were your 'sexual needs' never truly met or was it much broader than that? Perhaps a whole lot of other 'needs' were ignored, too (by you, your wife and society as a whole). It could have included your need for a fulfilling job, a meaningful life, spiritual fulfilment or just to feel valued for yourself (not as a cash machine that provided for the whole family). I can imagine you nodding your head as I went through the list. Sex is probably just the tip of the iceberg – and to be crude: the bit that sticks up above the water.

Once sex is just a pleasant pastime and a way to connect with your partner and no longer needs to make you feel whole, everything will look different. With the pressure off, you could talk honestly with your wife about sex (and your whole marriage) and have a different love life in this new marriage. But then, I guess you'll want to change a lot of other things too.

///////////////////////////////////////

Getting back the spark

In the last chapter, I explained my formula for what causes an affair:

Problem + Poor Communication + Temptation = Affair

We have covered the *problem* (in chapters Five and Six) and the *poor communication* (in Chapter Seven) but not the third element. So what about *temptation*? You might have been lucky and the discovery of your affair (and the jealousy your partner felt) has re-sparked your sex life. Many couples report having more sex and better sex than ever before. But what if your partner has been overwhelmed with flashbacks or thoughts of your affair partner every time the two of you have tried to make love? Perhaps the problem is with you. Maybe you don't fancy your husband or your wife any more and have no idea how to get the spark back.

Revisiting your sex life

A lot of unfaithful partners come to my office complaining that they might love their partner but they are not turned on by him or her. After a quick bit of detective work, I nearly always come to the same conclusion: I am not surprised. Time and again, there is a wall between the couple. The bricks are anger, resentment or being rejected over and over again. I tell them that resentment is the biggest passion killer. I explain that it is impossible to truly see each other, let alone feel a spark if there are a load of unresolved issues between the two of you.

What would happen if you talked honestly about your sex life, your desires and your disappointments? What would happen if you voiced your anger (by which I mean reporting it rather than acting out)? After all, your anger is just as valid as your partner's, your affair has not permanently put you in his or her debt, you can have needs and wants too. How would your feelings change if all your cards were on the table, rather than hiding the ones that you fear are unacceptable?

The next problem is that our society promotes all sorts of myths about sex, which makes it harder rather than easier for couples in long-term relationships to keep their love life alive — even if there hasn't been an affair. The three most dangerous are as follows:

Sex should happen spontaneously. I agree the best sex happens when by some magic the two of you are both relaxed and in the mood at the same time. However, if you rely on spontaneous sex you'd only have it three times a year – perhaps on your summer holiday, Valentine's Day and another occasion when all the stars align. I have a hard time convincing people, but there is nothing wrong with planning sex. So what are the advantages? It allows you to both arrive at the same place rested, washed (if that's important to you) and with the kids out of the way. If you don't feel in the mood when the sex date comes around, that's fine; you can have a bath together, give each other a massage, slow dance in the living room or reschedule.

A man's penis should be erect at all times during lovemaking. Once a man has an erection, he believes he has to use it. So a couple can skip foreplay and get down to 'business'. Unfortunately, it can mean that a woman is responding to her husband's desire rather than feeling her own. Furthermore, if you rush into sex, you don't explore a whole area of lovemaking which I call sensuality (and some people don't even consider it sex at all!). So what do I mean by sensuality? Basically, it is stroking, cuddling and intimacy which is not geared towards having an orgasm. For example, having a bath together and washing each other's hair, having a pillow fight or giving your partner a back rub.

Here's my main point: sensuality can be the gateway to sex AND it is a beautiful destination in its own right. So what about erections? I always tell men not to worry. Erections come and go. You don't have to cash every one in with an orgasm. In fact, holding onto the sexual energy and letting it simmer – perhaps for more lovemaking later – can be an extraordinary experience.

The better you know someone the easier sex is. I wish this one was true, but the better you know someone, the more your life is intertwined together and the higher the stakes. Rather than making it easier to show your true sexuality, we become frightened of being rejected or worried about upsetting our partner if we have a desire – however mainstream – that goes beyond the basic menu for sex. Time and time again, I help couples talk more honestly about simple ideas like dressing up, sex toys or making love in different places. Sadly, without my help they would have been unable to have these conversations. Sometimes I wonder if the number-one killer of sex lives in long-term couples is embarrassment. Especially after a period of not having much sex, discovering an affair and trying to reconnect again. Sure, it can be embarrassing. But remember, we accept the feelings and challenge the thoughts.

Hug till relaxed

I use this idea mainly for discoverers – especially if their partner touching them triggers pictures of affair sex. However, it can help you too – especially when you feel overwhelmed. So what is 'hug till relaxed' and how does it work? Most hugs are a quick in and out. Sometimes, it is more of a social hug and you lean forward so that only your shoulders touch. With 'hug till relaxed', you come completely together so each part of your body is touching. Take some deep breaths together, it really builds connection. And stay holding each other until you feel each other's bodies relax and melt into one another. It might take two minutes, it might take ten. It doesn't matter. When you're ready, you can talk about the trigger or the fears and decide whether to continue with being sensual and see what happens or talk some more.

More help

So what about temptation? There will always be attractive men and women and some of them might even throw themselves at you. However, if you have a satisfying and connected love life at home, the temptation will not be so strong. Especially if you have no outstanding problems that can't be talked about with your partner.

I could write a lot more about sex and long-term relationships. In fact, I already have. The book is called *Have the Sex You Want: A couple's guide to getting back the spark*. I also have a series of exercises both my team of therapists or myself can take you through to build connection and revolutionise your lovemaking. More details on my website.

Making amends with the children

When you started your affair, you thought it had nothing to do with your children and never considered the impact on them. So it has been a real shock to see just how much your children have been hurt.

A father's infidelity is particularly painful for teenage girls. They use their father as a safe space to flirt and try out their attractiveness. Your daughter has discovered sex can be dangerous, frightening and people get hurt. Teenagers of both genders have black and white views and will consider what you have done 'disgusting'. They are angry and will take sides.

Even if your children are older and have left home, they will still not want to think about their parents having sex (beyond enough times to conceive them) and suddenly – not to be crude – you have ground your sex life into their faces.

When Martin, forty-five, sought my help, one of the first things he told me about was a memory from when he was nineteen and discovered that his father was having an affair. 'Even though I had gone off to university, and should not have been as affected as my younger brother, I remember cycling round to my girlfriend's and making a promise to my future unborn children: I would never make the same mistake as my father and give them the pain he'd given me.' However, he didn't tell his father about his vow – or how much the threat of divorce had hurt him – until twenty-five years later after Martin had an affair himself. 'I explained about my vow on a walk in the woods and he literally had to stop to take in what I had said. He had no idea that I had lived my life in order to avoid being like him or how much his affair had hurt me. Despite a two-year period when my parents' marriage had been off and on, we had never once discussed it.'

So how can you mitigate the impact of infidelity on your children? The good news is that by helping your partner recover, you have started to acquire the skills to help your children. You know how to make a fulsome apology. You know how to acknowledge and accept anger rather than rescue. You need to do the same with your children. When they have finished talking and you have finished listening, you can apologise again.

Recently, I have been running workshops for men about facing the Father Wound (the impact of having a difficult relationship with your father). With really big groups – fifty-plus – I split them into smaller tribes of sons with different kinds of fathers: distant, dangerous, absent, critical, fearful, etc. Often the stories from the men in my workshops are far worse than their fathers having affairs (although that often comes up, too). Yet when I ask what they would most like to hear from their father each group comes up with the same core messages (which I think will resonate with your children too):

'Please forgive me.'

'I love you.'

'I am proud to be your father.'

'I'm here for you.'

'You are OK as you are.'

'I am sorry.'

I pass on these statements so you understand both the power of saying sorry and how much your children long to be heard and have their pain acknowledged. If they won't open up, tell them: 'I want to hear why you are angry' and listen and follow it up with: 'Tell me more.' If they still do not respond, respect their wishes. You will have opened up dialogue for the future. With time, your children will tell you how they are feeling.

EXERCISE: WHAT TO DO IF YOU STILL CAN'T DECIDE

In the first chapter, I suggested that if you couldn't decide whether to stay and work on your marriage or to leave and set up home with your affair partner, that you read the whole book. I hope that understanding why you were unfaithful, what a new relationship with your husband or wife could look like and how to achieve it have helped you make up your mind.

However, it is possible that you have gone through the book going 'Yes, but...' If you believe that you are different from the people in the book (and what applies to others doesn't apply to you), or you have decided that you deserve to be happy (and the other man or woman makes you happy) or I don't understand how you feel, then you have probably made your decision. I hope that reading this book and reaching this conclusion has been helpful.

If you're still undecided, I want to leave you with a few closing thoughts and some questions to ask yourself:

1. When you are under the influence of limerence, it is difficult to believe that it will not last for ever.

   Question: How do you know you are not getting a special offer from your affair partner to lure you in and that when you are committed normal service will be resumed?

2. If you have children, it is unlikely that they will forgive your affair partner for making their mother or father so unhappy and the best that you can hope for is a polite relationship with him or her. It is highly likely that they will be difficult and disruptive and cause stress in your new relationship. You will feel caught in the middle and one or both relationships will suffer.

   Question: How will each of your children respond to your divorce and how will it affect your relationship with each of them?

3. Although it feels like you only have two choices at the moment, there is a third one: to end both your marriage *and* your affair, and have some time on your own. Your wife and children will find this option less painful than going off with your lover.

   Question: How well would you cope with living on your own?

4. A brand new relationship has a greater chance of success than choosing your affair partner. Why should this be? When we are in a dark place, we tend to give off an energy that attracts other people dealing with similar material. So if you are unhappy and needing someone to save you (from your unhappy marriage), you are likely to find someone who also needs saving (from their unhappy marriage or an unhappy life). Two people needing saving is not a recipe for a successful long-term relationship.

   Question: What are the issues that your affair partner needs to face and how keen or prepared is he or she to do it?

5. On the open market, by which I mean single, you will have a greater and wider choice than when you are married (as many men and women would not consider opening their heart to someone who is either 'taken' or whose relationship status is 'complicated').

Question: Do you believe that you are lovable enough to attract someone else or can you not quite believe that your affair partner wants you?

However you answered these questions – as I discussed in Chapter One – it is important to take the truth drug (by which I mean being honest, open and transparent with everybody about your feelings). It will be painful but it is the only foundation for everyone in this complicated situation to move forward.

//////////////////////////////////////

Pulling everything together

When you started reading this book, you were lost and confused with no idea how to recover from your affair. If you did have a hazy idea of how to move forward, it seemed to be completely in your partner's gift (because he or she needed to forgive and move on). Now, I hope you understand why you were unfaithful, the personal issues that need to be addressed so you can lead a more fulfilled life, and the skills to resolve day-to-day problems with your partner. Unfortunately, the path to recovery is strewn with setbacks. Therefore, I am going to finish by highlighting the common mistakes and the qualities needed to avoid them.

Biggest mistakes in recovery

There are five issues I see time and again when people hit a wall:

➤ **Not being truly sorry.** You are angry about something but you are not expressing it – either for fear of how it will be received or because you feel it is not valid. What would happen if you were brave and acknowledged it first to yourself and then to your partner?

➤ **Not being empathetic enough.** If your partner feels you do not under-stand the depth of his or her pain, he or she will also question your love and commitment. If you don't understand something… ask.

➤ **Not combating stories told while still in Affair Brain.** In the early days, you will have been justifying your behaviour and told your partner something that you believed at the time. Although you have for-gotten it, the story has lodged deep in his or her brain (because it chimed with one of his or her greatest fears). So ask your partner if there is anything holding him or her back. Listen, ask questions, update with how you feel today and, finally, apologise again.

➤ **Not being truly committed (and covering it up).** It is OK to have doubts about recovery and express them. However, it's a problem when you pretend everything is all right and go into your shell or start up contact with the affair partner again.

➤ **Trying to live in the future.** Remember there are no shortcuts and attempting to skip ahead will frighten your partner and make him or her question whether you truly care.

Greatest assets in recovery

There are also five qualities that will help:

➤ **Honesty.** Taking the truth drug will lay the foundation for your part-ner to trust again and allow you to know yourself better.

➤ **Patience.** It is better to take your time and make a full recovery than sweep things under the carpet.

➤ **Curiosity.** It helps you look deeper and understand more.

➤ **Self-belief.** In the dark times, it is important to believe that you can change and grow.

➤ **Being a good listener.** Listening to your partner will also give you per-mission to listen to yourself.

SUMMARY

→ Trust comes at the end of the journey. It is not a prerequisite for starting it.

→ If you revitalise your lovemaking, the chances of being tempted again decrease sharply. It will also help your partner to believe in a future together.

→ A better and more connected relationship is within your grasp.

APPENDIX

//////

EMERGENCY HELP FOR DISCOVERERS

When something has triggered you in this book, please take a look at the following points:

➤ I am not blaming you for the affair.

➤ Your partner's affair is not your fault, whatever he or she might say.

➤ I am seeking to help your partner understand why he or she was unfaithful, so he or she can learn from his or her mistakes. I am not seeking to excuse.

➤ Even if your partner had legitimate complaints about your marriage, that is no reason to have an affair.

➤ Of course your partner should have spoken up about his or her problems (and maybe he or she did but in a way that was hard to hear or difficult to decipher). Perhaps your partner does not have the skills because he or she was brought up in a home where conflict was buried or it was too dangerous to face head-on.

➤ Affairs say more about the person who was unfaithful than their partner.

➤ It is normal to feel triggered (and it means nothing more than you are going through a hard time at the moment).

➤ What exactly triggered you? Have you mistaken your partner's rationalisation for his or her affair for some fundamental 'truth' about you or your relationship? For example: 'I wasn't satisfied at home.' What would happen if you challenged this idea? Is it your job to make your partner happy? What is his or her role in this task?

➤ Although your partner might have presented some 'reason' for his or her affair, it is most likely only the justification used to allow him or her to be unfaithful. This is *how* he or she cheated not *why*. I cover the differences in chapters four and five.

➤ Be kind to yourself and patient. It takes time to recover from an affair.

➤ I am not blaming you for your partner's affair. I have repeated this point because it can't be said often enough. Your partner is responsible for his or her choices NOT you.

This book was written for the partner who was unfaithful and if, in concentrating on their feelings, I have in any way offended you or not taken your pain seriously enough, I apologise. I have other books that are written especially for you: *How Can I Ever Trust You Again?* and *I Can't Get Over My Partner's Affair*. I also run an Infidelity Survival Training and Support Group with regular live events and targeted advice.

There are more details about all my work at my website: www.andrewgmarshall.com

Should I give this book to my partner?

In an ideal world, your partner would be pleased that you've gone to all the trouble of finding, reading and sharing a book to help him or her and your relationship. However, I'm well aware that he or she may have a totally different reaction. Perhaps your partner is too hurt or angry to listen, maybe he or she is hearing your overtures as criticism, or, alternatively, he or she thinks your relationship is beyond repair. So what should you do?

Obviously, it would be counter-productive to order him or her to read it; the chances of this happening are slight or he or she would open it with a closed mind. Please don't issue an ultimatum. For example: 'Read the book or leave.' It will put me, in your partner's mind, on your side. I need to remain neutral.

How to lay the ground

Whether your partner is relatively receptive or completely unco-operative, the following steps will maximise the chances of a positive conversation about this book.

Read the book yourself: It is much better to know what it's about than to guess. It could be that seeing you with it will make your partner curious and ask questions.

Don't rise to the bait: Your partner could easily be triggered by the title and go on the attack. For example: 'What does he know about me?' It will be tempting to get defensive but it will get you nowhere. Just say something non-committal: 'I am finding it helpful' or 'I'm learning a lot.'

Think about what you have learned: I would like this to be more about you than your partner. If you use my book to diagnose his or her problems, it will make him or her defensive. It's better for your partner to draw his or her own conclusions. However, I hope I'll have got you thinking about your life, why you do things and behaviours that you might like to change.

Find the right time to talk: You need to pick a neutral time – rather than just after a row. I would suggest waiting until you can have what is called a 'sideways discussion'. This is when you're doing something else and not facing each other – which can be confrontational. Good examples of sideways discussions would be when you're gardening together or on a long car journey. Under these circumstances, there are natural breaks in the conversation – so you can think or take a couple of deep breaths – and there is less chance of one or other of you wandering off.

Introduce the book: Communicate your learning about yourself and if you have made any changes that have reduced the temperature in your relationship, explain that they have come from reading this book. At this point, invite your partner to read it.

Listen to your partner: Rather than trying to counter your partner's doubts or using me to explain why you're right and he or she is wrong, nod your head. This will encourage your partner to say more. Ask an open question about something your partner has said. (Open questions start with how, why, what, when, who...) Use the three most useful words for communication: 'Tell me more.' You might find, your partner will begin to answer some of his or her doubts. More importantly, he or she will feel heard, that his or her opinions count and that you're not just trying to impose your solution.

What if my partner is not interested?

If your partner is not ready to read the book, please accept his or her decision. It is a 'no' for today, it does not mean 'no' for all time. It is important to remember this. Please don't read too much into the refusal either: it will be more about his or her shame and fears of being made to feel bad than 'love' for the affair partner or not being committed to recovery. However tempting it might be, don't use this book as a test. It is just a book and these are his or her feelings about it today. They could be different tomorrow.

If your partner refuses to work on your marriage, but you still love him or her, what are your options? I am always reminded of an old saying from my mother: 'You can lead a horse to water but you can't make it drink.' It doesn't mean that you have to stand idly by; you can continue to work on *your* recovery. Have a look at the books in the further reading section. From my books I would recommend: *Wake Up and Change Your Life: How to survive a crisis and be stronger, wiser and happier.* You could also consider getting personal therapy or joining a support group. If you change, it could change the dynamic between the two of you and make recruiting your partner to work on your marriage a real possibility.

However, if your partner is truly not open to change and is only interested in continuing to blame, you can also use this support network to look at your options and decide whether it is time to end the relationship.

FURTHER READING

The Drama of Being a Child by **Alice Miller** (Virago)
How the past can still affect us today.

Understanding and Treating Sex Addiction by **Paula Hall** (Routledge)
A non-judgemental look at the problems associated with compulsive use of pornography, visits to sex workers and multiple affairs.

Sex Addiction: The Partner's Perspective by **Paula Hall** (Routledge)
How partners can not only survive but also grow stronger and move on either in their relationship or alone.

Ninety Days: A Memoir of Recovery by **Bill Clegg** (Back Bay Books)
Understanding the ups and downs of recovery from addiction and the importance of support on the journey.

The Men on My Couch: True Stories of Sex, Love and Psychotherapy by **Dr Brandy Engler** (Berkley)
What lies behind men's focus on sex, what they really desire and what they most fear.

The Ethical Slut: A Practical Guide to Polyamory, Open Relationships, and Other Freedoms in Sex and Love by **Janet W. Hardy and Dossie Easton** (Ten Speed Press)
What is an open relationship and what is polyamory? A sensible and non-judgemental look at the complexities and possibilities of these arrangements.

Living an Examined Life: Wisdom for the Second Half of the Journey by **James Hollis** (Sounds True)

Daily meditations on the unfinished business of life and how it might still be haunting you.

Philosophy for Life (and other dangerous situations) by **Jules Evans** (Rider)
Twelve of the greatest philosophers from the ancient world sharing lessons on happiness and resilience.

No Mud, No Lotus: The Art of Transforming Suffering by **Thich Nhat Hanh** (Parallax Press)
When we know how to suffer, we suffer less: this is the claim from this leading Zen Buddhist teacher.

Waking Up: Searching for Spirituality without Religion by **Sam Harris** (Black Swan)
Author with a degree in neuroscience who follows no religion but believes Jesus, Buddha, Lao Tzu, Rumi and other sages have something important to teach us.

The Mystery Experience: A Revolutionary Approach to Spiritual Awakening by **Tim Freke** (Watkins Publishing)
Philosopher who combines both science and spirituality to help us know our 'deep self' and feel 'deep love'.

Why Buddhism is True: The Science and Philosophy of Meditation and Enlightenment by **Robert Wright** (Simon & Schuster)
How meditation can help us see clearly and gain a deeper and morally valid happiness.

Love and Limerence: The Experience of Being in Love by **Dorothy Tennov** (Scarborough House)
The classic study about limerence from the woman who coined the term. It explains love, infatuation, madness and all the flavours in-between.

The Four-Fold Way: Walking the Paths of the Warrior, Teacher, Healer, and Visionary by **Angeles Arrien** (Harper One)
How the spiritual approaches of other cultures can be useful for ours.

OTHER BOOKS BY ANDREW G. MARSHALL

I Love You But I'm Not in Love With You
Over 100,000 copies sold worldwide. This book will help you get to the roots of why seemingly loving partners detach and how the simple everyday things you thought were protecting your relationship were really undermining it. Also includes:

➤ More information about limerence.

➤ How to argue productively and address the core of the issue.

➤ Employ the trigger words for more effective communication.

➤ Find a balance between being fulfilled as an individual and being one half of a couple.

➤ Create new bonds instead of searching for old ones.

Have The Sex You Want
If your sex life is more about going through the motions than building connection, this book is for you. It features my step-by-step guide to bringing back the intimacy into your relationship and having the more connected sex you have always dreamed about. It also includes:

➤ Deal with different levels of desire.

➤ Combat the unhelpful myths about men and women and sex.

➤ Repair the damage from an affair by reconnecting again in the bedroom.

Wake Up and Change Your Life

I have nine ideas that build into a proven plan for personal transformation (which in turn could transform your relationship). Several of these ideas will be familiar as I have used some of the mantras in this book too. Most important, for when you're in crisis, there's advice on how to keep calm. The book also features:

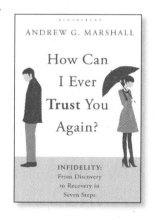

➤ Everything you need to know about improving the way you communicate.

➤ The importance of boundaries for you and your relationships.

➤ Understanding the difference between your zone of concern and your zone of control.

➤ An in-depth explanation about Mindfulness and living in the present.

How Can I Ever Trust You Again?

If you are struggling through the seven stages of recovery, there is help and advice in my classic book. It will help him or her make sense of all your feelings and reassure that they are normal and understandable. There's also my detailed plan on how to come out of this crisis with a stronger and better marriage. Each chapter ends with a short section written for the partner who has been unfaithful and many couples find these prompt, constructive conversations on how to move forward helpful. The book also includes:

➤ The eight types of affairs and how understanding your partner's is key to rescuing your relationship.

➤ How to stop your imagination running wild and your brain going into meltdown.

➤ How the person who had the affair can help their partner recover.

➤ What derails recovery and how to get your marriage on track again.

It's Not a Midlife Crisis, It's an Opportunity

If your life no longer makes sense and you're looking to make big changes, it will help you take stock, understand how you got to this place and make a considered plan for the future. Whether it is you or your partner who is traversing the mid-life crisis, this book offers:

➤ A whole new vocabulary for discussing the midlife crisis without alienating each other.

➤ What causes depression and what is a helpful and an unhelpful reaction.

➤ Five killer replies to the blocks that stop you talking properly about your marriage.

➤ Why if you pass the midlife test everything is up from here.

The Happy Couple's Handbook:
Powerful life hacks for a successful relationship

Love needs skills as well as chemistry. In this positive book, I have plenty of exercises and examples to help turn your relationship from an OK into a happy one. It includes:

➤ The rules for constructive arguments.

➤ How to be a better listener.

➤ Use carrots rather than sticks.

➤ How to forgive and move on.

My Memoirs

For periods during my midlife crisis, I kept a diary of which I have published two volumes and am working on a third.

My Mourning Year: A Memoir of Bereavement, Discovery and Hope

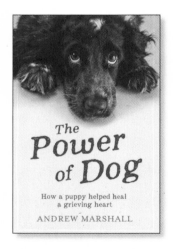

The Power of Dog: How a puppy helped heal a grieving heart

ABOUT THE AUTHOR

Andrew G. Marshall is a marital therapist with thirty-plus years' experience. He trained with RELATE (The UK's leading couple counselling charity) but now leads a team in private practice in London and Berlin offering the Marshall Method. He is also the author of twenty-one other books on relationships and contributes to *Mail on Sunday*, *Sunday Telegraph*, *Times* and women's magazines around the world. To date, his work has been translated into twenty different languages. You can follow Andrew on Twitter, Pinterest and Facebook, but to receive regular updates about his books, articles and events, subscribe to his newsletter at www.andrewgmarshall.com.